GROW THROUGH PRAYER

BY NECHAMA DINA WASSERMAN LABER

ART BY CHANA LABER

GROW Through Prayer

ISBN 979-8-218-07771-6

First Edition - Elul 5782 / September 2022

A project of Jewish Girls Unite & The GROW Connection Network
5 Mannix Rd
East Greenbush, NY 12061
www.JewishGirlsUnite.com
www.GrowConnectionNetwork.com

Layout by Carasmatic Design - www.carasmaticdesign.com

Printed in the USA

Dedicated in loving memory of

CHAYA BAS
HACHAZZAN YAKOV V'ESTHER

CLAIRE KOSDEN-PERSKIE

by her loving children

MICKI & NORMAN MASSRY

and their beloved children

JULIE AND JIM, MURRAY AND MALLORY,
LAURIE AND KEN AND THEIR FAMILIES.

Claire was a Holocaust survivor who embodied
connection with her loved ones and faith throughout her life.
Inspired by her legacy, JGU welcomes women of all
backgrounds to join the GROW Connection Network.

Dedicated to My Dear Children

CHANA & MENACHEM
YITZCHOK & DEVORA LEA
MINDELEAH & SIMCHA
KAYLA MIRIAM & MENDY

*May your lives be filled with peace and love,
bringing more light into this world.
May you all be showered with blessings
and kindness from the One above.*

יהי רציין שימולא ה' את
כל משאלות לבכם לטובה

באהבה,
Mommy

---

*Dedicated to the three special
women in my life who are
growing Torah homes and
raising the next generation of
Women of Valor:*

SHOSHANA WOLF

ELLIE WEINBERGER

& ALIZA LEANSE

-Shaindel Leanse

---

*In loving memory of
my dear mother in law,*

SARAH BAS BINYAMIN

and in honor of my grandchildren,

YOSEF GERSHON MEIR
& SHIRA MENUCHA

*I am grateful for my mother in law's
modeling of unconditional love and
so grateful I can pass this on to my
grandchildren! I recognize Hashem's
guidance and benevolence in my life.
I strive to learn and grow in oneness with
Hashem. I wish to share what I've learned
with as many people as possible with love
and inspiration.*

–Karen Sarto

Dedicated in Loving Memory of

FAIGA BAS BETZALEL MENACHEM MENDEL BASSMAN

by Dr. Reuvain & Shoshana Fox

Dedicated to my father,

RABBI AZRIEL YITZCHOK
BEN YISROEL WASSERMAN

*a devoted educator who modeled
the meaning of prayer.*

YARTZEIT 4 MENACHEM AV

Saved from the Flames

In a GROW Workshop for Educators in August 2021, I shared the following story:

As the GROW Method™ was being developed and I realized it really works, my mother brought me this photograph of my father, Rabbi Azriel Yitzchok Wasserman praying.

When my father passed away in 1985 at the age of thirty-seven, my mother gave family friend and artist Chaya Pellin the photo to create a painting that now hangs on my wall. Somehow, Chaya never returned the original photo and held onto it for all these years.

Notice the scorched border. Chaya's entire house burned and she unfortunately lost thousands of her paintings. A few survived — and this photo.

I knew my father was giving us a powerful message of hope. Look at him holding the *Siddur* as the fire is literally to his *Tallit*. How are we going to get through the challenges of our times? We are going to share the gift of a growing connection with Hashem every day. When we hold onto the *Siddur* and find our soul-space, we can pull ourselves out of despair. We can grow through pain and turn it into a prayer.

Perhaps I have been through my own loss in order to guide others to GROW through pain. My father's appreciation for each word of prayer inspires me to develop methods to make *Tefillah* more meaningful. Now, I would say that by connecting my daily agenda to *Tefillah* with the GROW Method™, Hashem is with me throughout my day.

CONTENTS

Author's Note

GRATITUDE - RECOGNITION - ONENESS - WISHES

"I am **Grateful**, *Modeh Ani*," are the first words we recite every morning. "I give thanks to You, living and eternal King, for You have mercifully returned my soul..." The Lubavitcher Rebbe added, "G-d believes in you and put you on earth with a distinct and unique mission: to bring G-d's light into your corner of the universe."

Gratitude grows into **Recognizing** Hashem's blessings in the details of our lives and the Divine Providence which guides our every step. I recognize how the Rebbe's words empowered my husband and me to embark on our unique mission to light up a corner of the world in Upstate NY in 1998. We founded the Capital Region Bat Mitzvah Club with the blessings of the head Shliach, Rabbi Israel Rubin. This "seed" grew into the Jewish Girls Retreat, the Jewish Girls Unite global community, and the new **GROW Connection Network**.

In **Oneness** with Hashem and with gratitude to our generous supporters, we are growing connections to our core, Creator, and community of alumnae, women, educators and leaders worldwide. Through our GROW Method™, multiple publications, online JGU programs, GROW Connection Circles, coaching, trainings and retreats, the Network offers resources and tools to nurture spiritual and emotional growth in ourselves and in the next generation.

I **Wish** for you to awaken each morning with gratitude and recognition for the overflowing blessings. May you have the strength to fulfill the mission you were born to accomplish and grow each day. I wish to welcome you to our global network and invite you to share the GROW Method™ and this book with your circle. May our efforts to GROW connections ensure a vibrant Jewish future, with our deepest wish for personal and collective redemption, speedily in our days.

Nechama Dina Wasserman Laber
JGU Global Director, Publisher & Author

Four Steps to GROW

The GROW Method™ is based on the four main steps of prayer to inspire meaningful connections with one's core, Creator, and community to nurture spiritual and emotional growth.

One can use the GROW Method™ to generate love and connection by practically applying the four, core steps of *Tefillah*, or prayer, found in the *Siddur*, or prayerbook. The literal meaning of *Siddur* in Hebrew is "order." Our Sages composed the text of prayer in a precise order of steps as a sort of G.P.S. directing us to our destination: a deep connection with Hashem, which is the true meaning of "*Tefillah*."

The acronym G.R.O.W. represents for the following steps of *Tefillah*:

- **G**RATITUDE

  Corresponding to *Birchos Hashachar*, the Morning Blessings

- **R**ECOGNITION

  Corresponding to *Pesukei Dezimra*, the Verses of Praise, a series of Psalms preceded by the blessing *"Baruch She'amar"* and followed by *"Yishtabach."*

- **O**NENESS

  Corresponding to the *Shema*, affirming G-d's Oneness

- **W**ISHES

  Corresponding to the *Shemoneh Esrei - Amidah*

Here is how one can apply these four steps to grow connection through prayer based on the structure of the *Siddur*. ***Ready, set, GROW!***

- ### Gratitude

This focuses on the PERSON and acknowledges our dependence on
Hashem for our existence. While we tend to worry, run and react, instead
we first express gratitude to Hashem for all of our blessings, starting with
the soul He restores to us daily.

I am Grateful for my...

- ### Recognition

We recognize Hashem through His providence, creations and miracles in
our world, or what we admire in others, and describe the wonder in vivid
detail. Focus on the here and now — even the 'little things': A soothing
cup of tea, sunshine streaming through the window, the considerate
gesture of a coworker. The antidote to anxious overstimulation is training
our brains to notice everything that's going right.

I Recognize the good in Hashem's wondrous world...

- ### Oneness & Ownership

We identify our goal or mission to reveal the Oneness of Hashem in
ourselves, the world and with others. In partnership with Hashem, we
take responsibility to own our steps towards success and embrace our
G-d given gifts and experiences to help us.

I pledge to reveal oneness (unity) with [my soul/my Creator/others] by...
I love Hashem with all my heart (emotions), my soul (my life) and my
possessions (passions). I am one with Hashem in my emotions and
actions by...

- ### Wishes

While expressing our desires can feel intimidating, we now articulate our
Wishes to Hashem, describing what we want that only He can provide,
in order to fulfill our mission that only we can do. We ask to achieve our
goals and enjoy the fruits of our efforts.

My wish is...

GROW *in Action!*

Be inspired to personally apply the GROW Method™ with real examples of women and girls who are consciously practicing this beautiful tool in the daily moments of life.

Nechama Laber: Preparing for the Jewish Girls Winter Retreat…

Good morning! Every day is a reason to celebrate and reach for the sun and the wonders that G-d gives us! Every morning, as I open my eyes, I thank G-d that I am able to say my Tefillah. I was resting and filling myself with energy to greet our winter retreat staff. I was thinking, "I'm not ready! I'm so tired!" Then I switched to GROW.

I am Grateful to be hosting our 15th winter Retreat in our own location. I opened my eyes to Recognize my sons who are keeping busy, my daughters Shaina and Raizel who prepared dinner and the beds, my Rivkah who decorated and watched Yosef Chaim, Chana who went to 5 stores for supplies, my husband who is picking up girls from airports and bus stations. Baruch Hashem, they even let me rest while this was happening after a day of coaching and teaching. In Oneness, Hashem is our partner. It's all for Him to empower our girls to connect and grow with love. I Wish for everyone to be healthy and happy and united to ignite beautiful souls in healthy bodies! I'm up and ready! Ready, set, GROW!

Anonymous: On the passing of my father as it was starting to sink in…

I am so Grateful for all the amazing years we had together; that I was able to be with him and hold his hand while he said goodbye to this world; for all my friends that love and support me; that I was able to say Shema with my father a few nights in the hospital and that David and my mom and sister were also with him. I Recognize that Hashem has his hand in everything and it isn't for me to try to understand or reason it out. That is above me and im yirtzeh Hashem, all will be revealed. I am One with Hashem, turning to him and leaning on Him completely. I Wish that no one else would feel this suffering of losing a loved one, a parent, a child, and for our lives to only be filled with love.

Nechama Laber: My Rebbe...

Today is the anniversary of the day my spiritual guide, the Rebbe of Chabad, accepted the leadership back in 1951. I'm Grateful for the moments as a teen, and when the Rebbe gave me the gift of his teachings in the form of farbrengens and booklets from his holy hand into mine. I Recognize that each lesson I learn from my Rebbe is a match to fuel my inner fire, my soul, each day. I am in Oneness when I share the light with others. Our soul is an inner flame always striving higher and yearning for Oneness. On this auspicious day, my soul Wishes to reach higher and create more vessels for this infinite light to share with our world.

Anonymous: One busy Erev Shabbos...

I'm tuning into my thoughts that keep directing me to resentment today. Instead, I am Grateful for GROW, for my stunning family, their support, my granddaughter and my health. I Recognize my husband's willingness to stay up with our granddaughter so I could sleep last night while we babysat her. I recognize how my kids care for me and each other so affectionately and are tuned into each other. I own my role as their mother and am One with Hashem, trusting that all my needs are met without me using control or anger. I Wish for a peaceful Erev Shabbos and to be present with my family.

From a mother dealing with a teenage girl...

I am Grateful she's discovering herself as a woman with desires to build a future family and for the women in her life who are supporting her growth. I Recognize the presence of a new baby as an impetus for deep life discussions and that my growth in the last months gave me the tools to guide my daughter to develop patience and self-discipline and see the beauty of a healthy, supportive marriage. I am One with Hashem in parenting my children; I own my part of purifying my intentions for raising my children. I Wish for my will to be Hashem's will and for Him to hold me through the process. My daughter will receive all she needs from me and the others we choose to surround her with. May she be inspired and strengthened to listen to her inner voice and compass.

Tzipporah Prottas: A junior educator and camp counselor's GROW

I am Grateful to Hashem and parents for the honor and trust they place in us to help shape their daughters' minds and souls. I Recognize the Divine spark in each girl that grants her inherent worth and dignity; so, I strive to treat her accordingly. I am One with Hashem by embracing the abilities He's equipped me with to share His Torah amid both joys and challenges, which all come from Him. I Wish for the insight, creativity, and energy to impart Torah in a meaningful and compelling way for the girls.

Nechama Laber: A special Yahrzeit Shabbos with my grandchildren…

On the Friday night that we celebrated my father's 74th birthday, I told my oldest grandson, named Azriel, about his Zaidy Azriel. I sang a song composed in my father's memory: "Kuk nisht oif der vei kuk oif di gezunt / See the good my love and trust the One above!" My son Yosef Chaim, who sat on my lap, started laughing and kissing me as if he understood this song was special.

I'm so Grateful for a beautiful Shabbos with my daughter Chaya's family and for the years that my father taught us about being an authentic Jew, dedicated teacher and father. I Recognize that we don't understand Hashem's ways and why my father passed away at 37 years old. Yet, 37 years later I see that his energy is still with us. In Oneness, I will continue to connect to my father's legacy through raising my children and teaching my students with the values he and my mother instilled in me. I Wish that my children, grandchildren and students follow in his footsteps. May he shower blessings for health and happiness from above; may we finally be reunited in person with the resurrection with the redemption, speedily in our days.

GROW with JGU Student Rochel Leah…

I am Grateful for my amazing friends in school, who support me and help me with a smile whenever I need it. I Recognize that Hashem is always with me and guiding me even in hard times. I am One with Hashem by learning for Chidon and making a strong connection with Him, even if it's hard and I'm not in the mood. I Wish to pass all the Chidon tests and for us all to see each other in Yerushalayim right now!!!

Anonymous: A change of travel plans…

This morning my plans to travel to a wedding were changed due to black ice. Though I was disappointed, I had an opportunity to practice GROW.

I'm Grateful to Hashem for being alive and not out on the road. I Recognize that Hashem runs the world and weather. I am One with Hashem in following His lead for my day. I am open to where Hashem wants me today. I Wish to celebrate many more Simchos in good health. L'Chaim!

From a woman going in for a medical exam…

Today, while at an appointment, I wasn't happy to be there and I've often canceled. So, I decided to try GROW while waiting.

Gratitude: Hashem made me a woman; we have technology and medicine to use to keep our bodies healthy; health insurance covers this expense. Recognition: Hashem gave us the ability to invent this technology. He made the world with all kinds of people with different talents and skills so that we can take care of each other. He is keeping me alive and healthy in this moment. He provides for all my needs. Oneness: I am not alone; Hashem is with me as I'm having this test. I am connected to all women over 35 who need mammograms annually. The woman operating the machine is guided by Hashem. Thank G-d, she is caring and treating me like a valued person. Hashem is in her and in me. Wish: I want healthy test results and the discovery of a less painful method for screening breast cancer.

Nechama Laber: GROW on Erev Shabbos...

I am Grateful for our beautiful tradition of lighting Shabbos candles every Friday, 18 minutes before sunset. I Recognize we are connecting to the global chain of Jewish women from daughter to mother, all the way back to our Matriarch Sarah. In Oneness with my daughters, I light 13 candles, Baruch Hashem - one for each member of my family. This fire fuels our entire week. I pray for the strength to shine Hashem's light in a dark world. I pray for our children to be a light to the world. I pray for peace and healing for all humanity. This morning, I prepared my Shabbos candles by kindling and extinguishing the wicks. This makes them easier to light later on. When I prepare my vessels properly, I can bring in the light without stress. I Wish to usher in the light of Shabbos with joy and calm in loving memory of Mrs. Razel Wolvovsky, my dear friend Batya Rosenblum's beautiful mother.

From a member grateful to join the GROW Connection Circle...

I'm so Grateful that I found Nechama. I've gotten so much chizuk from her in the short time I've known her! I Recognize the Hashgacha Pratis, because I found her by Googling someone else I heard about. I found Nechama's name there and liked what I read! I feel closer to Oneness with Hashem through the lessons she is teaching and I Wish my daughters will learn from her, too!

GROW with JGU Student Adira...

Gratitude:

- For strength even when I'm tired!
- A warm house even when it is cold outside.
- A good night's sleep.
- That I have more than enough of everything I need, unlike many people.
- For a loving family that supports me with everything I do.
- A cute cat.
- A very nice comfortable bedroom that I can feel relaxed, let loose, and happy in!
- Good health even when everyone around me is getting sick and feeling hopeless.
- That Hashem has made a way to be forgiven for mistakes.
- The birds that chirp outside of my window letting me know a new day has come.

- A unique, fun, special, funny family!
- For friends that feel like family!
- That I live in a city with Jewish girls my age unlike before.
- That I have the chance to be on a Jewish girls basketball team!
- That my body works 100%
- That my mother cares so much about me and makes sure I am healthy and happy!
- A good school with friends and teachers who care about me and love me.
- For GROW because I now enjoy davening and look forward to it every day!

Recognition:

- That I can change my mood with my mindset!
- That GROW is helping me with real life situations!
- That Hashem is keeping me safe, healthy, and happy in this crazy and hopeless time.
- How Mrs. Laber puts so much effort into JGU/JGR in making it awesome and fun!
- How Mommy made winter break so fun and productive!
- How the weather forecast was wrong, and Hashem brought sunshine instead of rain.
- How everyone in my family supports me and loves me!

Oneness:

- Daven with more kavanah
- Say Tehillim in my free time
- Do a new Mitzvah that I don't normally do
- Remember after Berachos
- Try to be positive and focus on the more important stuff
- Try to be honest
- Try to help other people do Mitzvos
- Learn from mistakes
- Exercise
- Do something new
- Spend time with my family
- Kindness
- Recognize GROW in davening
- Find the good in others
- Be the best me I can be
- Helping others
- Don't compare myself to others
- Find times when Hashem just shows me through the little things that He loves me
- Be the girl who does the right thing even when no one knows or is looking

Wishes:

- Good health
- Shalom Bayis
- No stress
- Productivity
- Good weather
- Free time to do things I enjoy
- Opportunities to do new things
- Happiness
- Strength when I'm tired or upset
- A refreshing night of sleep

Come Into My Garden

Meditation ∼

Find yourself a comfortable position, close your eyes (if desired) and take a long, deep breath; hold it a second, and let it go. Do this a few more times.

Imagine yourself in a beautiful garden. Take in all the sights, sounds, smells, and feelings of this special place.

As you are enjoying this place, someone very special is coming toward you. It could be a wise mentor or teacher, a trusted friend, or someone in the Torah whom you admire. You greet each other, and you are told they have brought you something you have been wanting. You put out your hand to receive it, and it is a seed, a seed containing all the potential of some special quality or dream you have been wanting to cultivate.

Hold this seed in your hand... What kind of energy do you feel? Does it feel familiar or new to you? Does the seed tell you something about yourself that you didn't know?

Find a special place to plant this seed, a place with fertile soil, a place which you can easily return to. Dig a hole, just deep enough so the seed can easily sprout. Ask Hashem, your Creator, to bless you with what this seed needs to grow and blossom into its fullness and wholeness.

And as you cover this seed with rich, fertile soil, give yourself a blessing of how you desire its essence to blossom within you. Gently water this little seed and bathe it with your love and caring.

How will you take care of this little seed? What does it need to sprout and grow? How will it branch out? What kind of nurturing does it need? Who would you like to ask for help to nurture it? What will this seed be like when it matures? How will you be different?

Take a few minutes alone with your seed, and think about how you will nurture it and how you will blossom. We are trees with roots, branches and fruits. We bear fruits when we share our gifts with others so that they can plant seeds, too. May our sweet fruits blossom in Hashem's beautiful garden.

"כי האדם עץ השדה"

A Person is a Tree of the Field[1]

Meditation

by Chana Laber

Let your mind be your roots. Reaching down into earth, grounding you.

Your knowledge and thoughts become the water nurturing your thirst to know more and grow. The thoughts you choose builds your existence, growing into your heart.

What you feed your mind will grow into what you feel. Your emotions blossoming into branches, arms of action. How you feel will bring you to do. And your efforts will bear fruit.

Choose a thought. Imagine it traveling along this pathway. This is how I visualize a symbiotic relationship of "mind over heart." Where our mind is an incubator for growth.

The choices that we make, the things we see, think, learn, listen to, all marinate together. Sprouting into a feeling or emotion, which then causes even more growth, an action, a visible impact in our life. Our thoughts are so potent and powerful, what you feed your mind, that's what will grow.

Notice that if you turn this picture upside down it will follow the anatomy of a person. The brain on top, feeding the heart, spreading to all parts of our body, our arms and legs are the branches, the parts of ourselves that create and take action.

---

1. *Devarim 20:19*

Ready, Set, GROW! 〜

G: Gratitude = My Roots

"I am grateful for my roots: my soul, faith and trust, my family, parents, grandparents, foremothers and forefathers."

R: Recognition = My Trunk

"I recognize the ways Hashem sustains my life."

O: Oneness = My Branches

"I dedicate my life to growing Oneness with *Hashem,* so I can branch out into the world through my emotions and actions and by sharing my G-d-given gifts in the service of Torah and *Mitzvos*."

W: Wishes = My Fruits, Hashem's Blessings

"I wish for Hashem's blessings for my actions to bear fruits and impact others. I wish for rain, or "*geshem,*" which also means "*gashmiyus -* physicality" to sustain my spiritual mission."

May blessings shower down on you. May you grow to be fruit-bearing trees.

Reflect & Connect 〜

Fill in the roots of your tree with gratitude.

Fill in the trunk with detailed recognition for the ways Hashem sustains you.

Fill in the branches with your goals and the ways you branch out and express yourself each day, in Oneness with Hashem.

Fill in the fruits with your wishes for the impact of your actions.

Spiritual Sunshine Meditation

Find a comfortable position.

Notice the sensations of your breathing:

The rise and fall of your chest,

The air entering your lungs,

The release of each exhale.

Allow yourself to be refreshed with each breath.

Visualize yourself in Hashem's garden;

Turn your attention to the rising sun

Shining brightly in the sky.

"And it was night… and it was morning…" (Bereishis 1:5)

Take in all aspects of the sun showering you with its golden rays.

The sun's rays are sending you stamina and strength.

Feel the relief of the sunbeams

Drawing all negativity out of your body.

Feel the heat of the sun

Melting all tension off your muscles;

Any tightness is bathed in the glow of the sun.

The sunshine fills you with courage and bravery

This sunshine is within you at all times.

It is glowing brighter than ever in your eternal and internal landscape.

Like the sun, your soul rises each morning.

Breathe in and exhale.

Let go of anything that stands in the way of letting your soul shine.

Breathe in joy, laughter, happiness;

Breathe out any and all negativity.

Breathe in energy, vitality, stamina;

Let go of fatigue.

Feel the gentle rise and fall of your chest.

Move your body in any way that feels good.

Feel the warmth of your soul.

Your soul is ready to shine bright.

when you
PLOW & SOW
things will
GROW

GROW THROUGH PRAYER

Selections from the Siddur
illuminated by art and reflections

STEP 1: GRATITUDE

A builder knows that without a solid base, an entire structure is worthless. Start your day with gratitude. This is the foundation for your day and for your success. Be grateful for what you already have while you pursue your goals to build the future. If you aren't grateful for what you already have, what makes you think you'd be happier with more?

MODEH ANI

מוֹדֶה אֲנִי לְפָנֶיךָ מֶלֶךְ חַי וְקַיָּם שֶׁהֶחֱזַרְתָּ בִּי נִשְׁמָתִי בְּחֶמְלָה, רַבָּה אֱמוּנָתֶךָ

I give thanks to You, living and eternal King, for You have mercifully
returned my soul (breath of life) within me; great is Your faithfulness.

Good Morning, world.

The fiery sun has risen and a new day beckons.

"*Modeh Ani...*" I thank my eternal King for my soul.

Like a flame, it flickers upward, striving to GROW!

It fills me with fiery passion to fulfill my goal.

I am grateful for my Divine soul with infinite worth.

I am a powerful, positive force of light.

Like the sun, my soul illuminates the earth.

Ki ner Hashem Nishmas Adam.[2]

I am a flame.

Why are we allowed to recite *Modeh Ani* before we wash our hands, when
we may not otherwise pray?

The *Hayom Yom* for Shevat 11 teaches: "*Modeh Ani*" is recited upon
awakening and before washing the hands, even while we are 'impure.'
All the impurities in the world do not defile a Jew's soul. We are always
connected to Hashem.

---

2. "The soul of a person is the candle of Hashem." -King Solomon's Proverbs, 20:27

Meditation

Modeh Ani...
Breathe in and feel the soul that Hashem breathed into you.
Breathe out and release all worry and tension.
Breathe in gratitude for being alive.
Breathe out and release fear or doubts.
Breathe in the light of your soul.
It is striving to soar higher.
Breathe out fear of growth.
As you breathe, close your eyes and listen to the voice of your Neshama.
Listen to what she is saying.
How does she want to grow?

You Are a Flame
Poem by Malkah Reisner

You are a flame of shining light
Reflected from your soul
And when the world around you sees
Your rays affect their own
You leave a mark of light
That they carry just within
It's the fuel for their own spark
To carry on and grow

You illuminate such power
The fire from your soul
A flame that never wavers
It touches all you know

And the hardest thing to show you
Is your flame you carry high
You don't even know how great
Is the power of your light

The Gift of Gratitude

by Terri Klein, from her book *Life Unwrapped*

*Thank You for the morning light,
and for allowing me to survive the night.*

*Thank You for helping me to rise.
I will use good judgment and try to be wise.*

*And even if the sun won't shine,
I will own today and make it mine.*

*Thank You for the gift of my health,
as this, by far, defines my wealth.*

*Thank You for the gift of my smile.
Oh, and thank You, Dear G-d, for letting me stay a while.*

*I can walk, dance, sing, and laugh,
oh, lucky me.
I can feel, hear, smell, touch, and such beauty I can see.*

*What an abundance of blessings surround
that are just waiting to be found.*

*My heart swells with thanks, and I promise today
to do my very best, in every possible way.*

*I will spread the magic of life
to deal with both the sweet and the sour,
because every day is precious,
as is every hour.*

*Because it is borrowed, my time here on Earth,
I plan to use it wisely, for all that it's worth.*

*Considering we live in a clock-eyed world,
it's my duty to slow the pace,
so I will smell the flowers, cherish the beauty,
and savor every taste.*

*Time is a treasure
that cannot be bought or sold.
We each have twenty-four hours
in a day to hold.*

*It's how I choose to use mine
that defines me,
so I will cherish life and be of service to others,
you will see.*

*I will live, love, laugh;
I will not yell; I will make it a sin,
for in yelling, no one wins
and more problems only begin.*

*I will appreciate the simple pleasures
that transport my soul,*

all the miracles of nature
that complete me and make me
whole.

Like a beautiful garden, a radiant
sunset,
a gentle hug, a smile, or even just a
kind word,
it is often the silent gestures that
mean the most,
although they cannot be heard.

Life is a precious gift to be gratefully
unwrapped,
and there is so much to celebrate.
So I will no longer wait; it is the here
and now, today,
that I will celebrate and appreciate.

It is said that every crisis faced
together
makes the circle more strong and
tight.
It is my own personal experience
that has proven this to be right.

From life's challenges and obstacles
come optimism, inner strength, and
personal growth.
It is the tough times that teach us the
lessons
We need to learn the most.

Thank You for my freedom,
and for helping to co-create my
vision.

I hope You are happy
with my choices and my mission.

Most importantly, I thank You
for my ever-so-precious family and
friends,
who understand my philosophy
and will stick by me till the end.

I promise to make people feel special,
each and every day.
It is my commitment to leave people
better than I found them,
for this is my only way.

So off I go to start my day, Dear G-d,
I hope to make You proud.
For just to be alive and well is such a
blessing,
another chance at the here and now.

Please allow me
to be of service to You.
I look forward to Your guidance,
my whole life through.

Forever Grateful for the Gift of Today

Ready, Set, GROW!

- I am grateful for my soul being renewed and refreshed today, giving me the power to grow.

- I am grateful to Hashem for His unconditional love, which is not conditional on what I do.

- I am grateful to Hashem for giving me a Jewish soul with a unique mission. Although I have a huge debt of unpaid bills to my Creator, nevertheless He continues to return my collateral back to me, refreshed for daily use.

- I am grateful to You, Hashem, for choosing me to serve You. I am grateful to awaken from the emptiness of the world to the true reality that I stand before Hashem — King of all kings — ready to fulfill my mission.

- I am grateful for a new day and a new beginning!

Reflect & Connect

מוֹדֶה אֲנִי - I Give Thanks

In Hebrew, a Jew is called *Yehudi*, from the word "*Yehuda*," similar to the word "*Modeh*," which means thanks and acknowledgment. The definition of a Jew is one who is grateful.

Leah *Imeinu* named her fourth son Yehuda to express her appreciation for his birth. She did not take his birth for granted.

רַבָּה אֱמוּנָתֶךְ - Great is Your Faithfulness

Hashem has greater faith in us than we have in ourselves; He has faith in us to fulfill the purpose for which we were created. He returns our soul each morning with the strengths we will need for the day. When we trust in Hashem, we can accept our mission with the confidence that He will guide our every step.

How does Hashem have faith in you? How do you show your faith in Hashem?

Our Sages taught us to say: "בשבילי נברא העולם The world was created for me" and "I was created to serve my Creator." In other words, the world was created for me to fulfill a purpose, using my G-d-given gifts and innate strengths.

How does humility fit with the above idea? Humility means that we acknowledge that all of our blessings and strengths are gifts from Hashem to fulfill our mission.

How can you motivate yourself to jump out of bed in the morning?

Start your day right by setting an intention. What is your intention today?

NETILAS YADAYIM

Immediately after reciting *Modeh Ani,* one pours water over the hands up to the wrist, alternating three times, right then left, without a blessing. This water is prepared in a cup and basin and set beside one's bed before going to sleep the previous night.

It is preferable for one to wash the hands before moving four cubits, or six feet, from one's bedside. Otherwise, wash at the first available opportunity. Before washing the hands, avoid touching clothing, food, and openings of the body, or reciting blessings and prayers, due to the spiritual impurity that rests on the hands from sleep.

After using the restroom and dressing, now in a more presentable state of mind and body, one pours water over the hands from a vessel a second time, following the same procedure and reciting:

בָּרוּךְ אַתָּה יְהֹוָה אֱלֹהֵינוּ מֶלֶךְ הָעוֹלָם
אֲשֶׁר קִדְּשָׁנוּ בְּמִצְוֹתָיו וְצִוָּנוּ עַל נְטִילַת יָדָיִם:

Blessed are You, Hashem, our G-d, King of the Universe, Who sanctified us with His commandments and commanded us to wash [literally: elevate] the hands.

The Hebrew word "*netilat*" rather than the typical word "*rochatz*" is used to refer to the washing, because "*notal*" also means to "raise and uplift." This hints to the holiness of the handwashing, which symbolizes how we 'lift up' or dedicate the work of our hands to Hashem, the King of all Kings.

Meditation

We are called a "Kingdom of priests (kohanim) and a holy nation."[3]

Envision the kohanim in the Holy Temple purifying themself with the holy waters of the copper washstand called the Kiyor. Their image is reflected in the Kiyor made of the holy mirrors donated by the courageous Jewish women in Egypt. Despite their difficult circumstances, these women did not give up: They beautified themselves with their mirrors and inspired their husbands to continue raising families. Together, they built the Jewish future. They are giving you strength today to break out of your personal Egypt to build your bright future and the future of our people.

---

3. *Shemos 19:6*

You are a kohen in your mini sanctuary for Hashem. Are you ready to fulfill your mission? Are you ready to elevate the world with the work of your hands? What or who will you elevate today?

Ready, Set, GROW!

- I am grateful for my hands to serve like the priestly *Kohanim* in my own Sanctuary.

- I am grateful to elevate the world with my hands and fulfill my unique mission.

- I am grateful to wash away negativity as I begin my day.

Reflect & Connect

While your body rests, your soul ascends heavenward to recharge. This resulting void allows for a negative spiritual state called *"tumah."* Upon awakening, we wash away the unclean spirit left on the nails and restore purity to our body and mind. We begin our day by washing away negativity or impurities.

What spiritual negativity will you wash away?

ASHER YOTZAR

בָּרוּךְ אַתָּה יְהֹוָה אֱלֹהֵינוּ מֶלֶךְ הָעוֹלָם אֲשֶׁר יָצַר אֶת הָאָדָם בְּחָכְמָה וּבָרָא בוֹ
נְקָבִים נְקָבִים חֲלוּלִים חֲלוּלִים גָּלוּי וְיָדוּעַ לִפְנֵי כִסֵּא כְבוֹדֶךָ שֶׁאִם יִפָּתֵחַ אֶחָד
מֵהֶם אוֹ יִסָּתֵם אֶחָד מֵהֶם אִי אֶפְשַׁר לְהִתְקַיֵּם וְלַעֲמֹד לְפָנֶיךָ אֲפִילוּ שָׁעָה אֶחָת.
בָּרוּךְ אַתָּה יְהֹוָה רוֹפֵא כָל בָּשָׂר וּמַפְלִיא לַעֲשׂוֹת:

Blessed are You, Hashem, our G-d, King of the Universe, Who formed man with wisdom and created within him openings and hollows. It is obvious and known in the presence of Your glorious throne that if one of them were ruptured, or if one of them were blocked, it would be impossible to exist and stand in Your Presence even for a short while. Blessed are You, Hashem, Who heals all flesh and performs wonders.

Meditation

Openings and Hollows

Reflect on how the body and soul are miraculously unified; one needs the other to fulfill its purpose. Reflect on how Hashem sustains your body in wondrous ways. Caring for your body, the home for your soul, is an expression of gratitude to Hashem, Who preserves the breath of life within you.

Rabbi Tanchuma declared that if an inflated balloon has a hole the size of a needlepoint, it would lose all its air. However, the human body is full of openings, yet it does not lose the breath of life.

Ready, Set, GROW!

- I am grateful to You, Hashem, for giving me a body custom-designed with awesome wisdom.

- I am grateful to You for forming me with wisdom, for healing and for performing wonders.

- I am grateful for digestion, respiration and all normal bodily functions - Hashem's great wonders.

- I am grateful for my body, which is a tool to serve Hashem!

- I am grateful Hashem is aware of the mundane needs of each individual.[4]

Reflect & Connect

How do you practice self care and soul care?

---

4. *Vilna Gaon*

What is fascinating to you about the workings of the body?

How can you express gratitude with your five senses?

I am grateful I can taste...

I am grateful I can touch...

I am grateful I can see...

I am grateful I can hear...

I am grateful I can smell...

ELOKAI NESHAMA

אֱלֹהַי, נְשָׁמָה שֶׁנָּתַתָּ בִּי טְהוֹרָה הִיא אַתָּה בְרָאתָהּ אַתָּה יְצַרְתָּהּ אַתָּה נְפַחְתָּהּ
בִּי וְאַתָּה מְשַׁמְּרָהּ בְּקִרְבִּי וְאַתָּה עָתִיד לִטְּלָהּ מִמֶּנִּי וּלְהַחֲזִירָהּ בִּי לֶעָתִיד לָבֹא,
כָּל זְמַן שֶׁהַנְּשָׁמָה בְּקִרְבִּי מוֹדֶה אֲנִי לְפָנֶיךָ יְהוָה אֱלֹהַי וֵאלֹהֵי אֲבוֹתַי רִבּוֹן כָּל
הַמַּעֲשִׂים אֲדוֹן כָּל הַנְּשָׁמוֹת: בָּרוּךְ אַתָּה יְהוָה הַמַּחֲזִיר נְשָׁמוֹת לִפְגָרִים מֵתִים:

My G-d! The soul which You bestowed in me is pure; You created it, You formed it, You breathed it into me and You preserve it within me. You will eventually take it from me and restore it in me in the time to come.

So long as the soul is within me, I give thanks to You, Hashem, my G-d and G-d of my fathers, Master of all creatures, Master of all souls. Blessed are You, Hashem, Who restores souls to dead bodies.

Meditation

Stand in front of your mirror and talk to your magnificent self:
Breathe in and breathe out;
Breathe in Hashem's kindness (chesed), revealed blessings;
Breathe in Discipline (gevurah), the gifts He withholds for the right time;
Place your hands on your heart and breathe in compassion (tiferes).

You are a reflection of Hashem.
Hashem breathed a pure soul into you.
There is a part of Hashem in you.
Notice your body from head to toe.
Feel Hashem's love and light within you.
The pure soul is primary in your life.
Your soul has a unique purpose in this world.
There is no limit to what you can accomplish.
Loving Hashem means loving you.

Breathe in harmony and connection;
Breathe out lack and expectation.
Breathe in gratitude and joy;
Breathe out the "oy!"
Breathe in Hashem's love;
Breathe out fear and doubt.
It will all work out.
Feel the expansion of your mind, body, and soul.
Breathe in and breathe out.

Ready, Set, GROW!

- I am grateful to You for my pure soul that You breathed into me; it is a part of Hashem in me.

- I am grateful that You preserve it and restore souls to bodies.

Reflect & Connect

אַתָּה נְפַחְתָּהּ בִּי - **You breathed it [my soul] into me**

When you blow up a balloon, you breathe out from your deepest inner self. So too, our soul is Hashem's deep breath. The *Neshama* is truly a part of Hashem!

All living things were created alive, meaning their body and life force were created at the same time. In contrast, man was created in the image of Hashem. Hashem first formed man's body from the earth and then "breathed into his nostrils a living soul."[5]

וְאַתָּה מְשַׁמְּרָהּ בְּקִרְבִּי - **You preserve it within me**

Why does Hashem have to preserve our soul in our body?

Were it not for Hashem preserving our soul, it would fly out of our body and return to heaven. It has no interest in the world and it yearns to be close to Hashem. But the soul has to fulfill a mission upon this earth.

What is your soul's mission?

וְאַתָּה עָתִיד לִטְּלָהּ מִמֶּנִּי וּלְהַחֲזִירָהּ בִּי לֶעָתִיד לָבֹא - **You will eventually take it from me and restore it in me in the time to come**

This statement refers to the time when the deceased will be resurrected.

———————————

5. Bereishis 2:7

הַמַּחֲזִיר נְשָׁמוֹת לִפְגָרִים מֵתִים - **Who restores souls to dead bodies**

This is a reference to Hashem restoring the soul each morning following its departure while one sleeps.

How does this prayer strengthen your beliefs?

Draw the colors expressing your soul.

MORNING BLESSINGS

Having thanked Hashem for restoring our soul and maintaining our bodily health, we now thank Him for all that the body and soul require in order to serve together.

Blessed are You, Hashem, our G-d, King of the Universe, Who gives the rooster understanding to distinguish between day and night.

בָּרוּךְ אַתָּה יְהוָֹה אֱלֹהֵינוּ מֶלֶךְ הָעוֹלָם אֲשֶׁר נָתַן לַשֶּׂכְוִי בִינָה לְהַבְחִין בֵּין יוֹם וּבֵין לָיְלָה:

Blessed are You, Hashem, our G-d, King of the Universe, Who gives sight to the blind.

בָּרוּךְ אַתָּה יְהוָֹה אֱלֹהֵינוּ מֶלֶךְ הָעוֹלָם פּוֹקֵחַ עִוְרִים:

Blessed are You, Hashem, our G-d, King of the Universe, Who releases the imprisoned.

בָּרוּךְ אַתָּה יְהֹוָה אֱלֹהֵינוּ מֶלֶךְ הָעוֹלָם מַתִּיר אֲסוּרִים:

Blessed are You, Hashem, our G-d, King of the Universe, Who straightens the bent.

בָּרוּךְ אַתָּה יְהֹוָה אֱלֹהֵינוּ מֶלֶךְ הָעוֹלָם זוֹקֵף כְּפוּפִים:

Blessed are You, Hashem, our G-d, King of the Universe, Who clothes the naked.

בָּרוּךְ אַתָּה יְהֹוָה אֱלֹהֵינוּ מֶלֶךְ הָעוֹלָם מַלְבִּישׁ עֲרֻמִּים:

Blessed are You, Hashem, our G-d, King of the Universe, Who gives strength to the weary.

בָּרוּךְ אַתָּה יְהֹוָה אֱלֹהֵינוּ מֶלֶךְ הָעוֹלָם הַנּוֹתֵן לַיָּעֵף כֹּחַ:

Blessed are You, Hashem, our G-d, King of the Universe, Who spreads the earth above the waters.

בָּרוּךְ אַתָּה יְהֹוָה אֱלֹהֵינוּ מֶלֶךְ הָעוֹלָם רוֹקַע הָאָרֶץ עַל הַמָּיִם:

Blessed are You, Hashem, our G-d, King of the Universe, Who prepares the steps of man.

בָּרוּךְ אַתָּה יְהֹוָה אֱלֹהֵינוּ מֶלֶךְ הָעוֹלָם הַמֵּכִין מִצְעֲדֵי גָבֶר:

Blessed are You, Hashem, our G-d, King of the Universe, Who provided me with all my needs.

בָּרוּךְ אַתָּה יְהֹוָה אֱלֹהֵינוּ מֶלֶךְ הָעוֹלָם שֶׁעָשָׂה לִי כָּל־צָרְכִּי:

Blessed are You, Hashem, our G-d, King of the Universe, Who girds Israel with might.

בָּרוּךְ אַתָּה יְהֹוָה אֱלֹהֵינוּ מֶלֶךְ הָעוֹלָם אוֹזֵר יִשְׂרָאֵל בִּגְבוּרָה:

Blessed are You, Hashem, our G-d, King of the Universe, Who crowns Israel with glory.

בָּרוּךְ אַתָּה יְהֹוָה אֱלֹהֵינוּ מֶלֶךְ הָעוֹלָם עוֹטֵר יִשְׂרָאֵל בְּתִפְאָרָה:

Blessed are You, Hashem, our G-d, King of the Universe, Who did not make me a Gentile.

בָּרוּךְ אַתָּה יְהֹוָה אֱלֹהֵינוּ מֶלֶךְ הָעוֹלָם שֶׁלֹּא עָשַׂנִי גּוֹי:

Blessed are You, Hashem, our G-d, King of the Universe, Who did not make me a slave.

בָּרוּךְ אַתָּה יְהֹוָה אֱלֹהֵינוּ מֶלֶךְ הָעוֹלָם שֶׁלֹּא עָשַׂנִי עָבֶד:

Blessed are You, Hashem, our G-d, King of the Universe, Who removes sleep from my eyes and slumber from my eyelids.

בָּרוּךְ אַתָּה יְהֹוָה אֱלֹהֵינוּ מֶלֶךְ הָעוֹלָם הַמַּעֲבִיר שֵׁנָה מֵעֵינָי וּתְנוּמָה מֵעַפְעַפָּי:

Meditation

Wiggle your toes, feel your feet.
Feel the support of your seat.
Touch your heart; breathe in, breathe out.
Close your hands tightly.
Open them slowly and recite:
"I am grateful to receive Hashem's blessings today.
Hashem is directing every step of my way."

Ready, Set, GROW!

- I am grateful to You for the understanding to distinguish between day and night.

- I am grateful for the circadian rhythm, the internal bio-clock that keeps my body producing the right hormones at the right time.

- I am grateful that I opened my eyes. I can see an entire world out there!

- I am grateful I sat up in bed. My limbs are moving. I'm alive! I am grateful to Hashem for "releasing the bound," renewing my energy and freeing my soul from spiritual darkness each morning.

- I am grateful for my ability to stand up.

- I am grateful to be up and dressed.

- I am grateful I handed in my soul last night, weary and frustrated and the Master of All Souls returns it to me fresh and clean, with power to grow!

- I am grateful to You for the ground beneath my feet. The truth is, it's a totally quirky freak of nature that planet Earth has any dry land at all. Minerals are heavier than water, so they should all be submerged beneath a single, vast ocean.

- I am grateful to You that Hashem directs my steps. I'm walking forward. I'm where I am supposed to be, guided by His hand.

- I am grateful Hashem provides for all my needs, especially shoes which allow me to take the first step towards my goals. Everything I need awaits me. It's up to me to put on my shoes to go out there and get it.

- I am grateful for the strength to overcome my evil inclination.

- I am grateful that Hashem crowns me with beauty.

- I am grateful I am not a Gentile.

- I am grateful for my freedom.

- I am grateful Hashem removed sleep from my eyes.

(Adapted from Tzvi Freeman on Chabad.org)

Reflect & Connect

Expect Nothing, Appreciate Everything!

How does a chewy bagel with a hole connect with the morning blessings?

Start with nothing, and anything is fantastic. I have a soul, a body, I am alive! And then the next step: "Not only do I exist; I have food to eat for breakfast!" With that step, all of life becomes a celebration. Every detail of it.

The strategy is tested and proven. Take Alice Hertz-Sommer, who survived the Theresienstadt concentration camp and is still happily playing Bach at 108—all because of that grateful-for-anything attitude. This was her motto: Life is a Gift!

When I focus on what I have instead of what is lacking, I feel grateful. When I feel grateful, I feel joyful. The returns of gratitude are as endless as the circle of the bagel.

(Adapted from "Gratefulness and the Holy Bagel" by Tzvi Freeman for Chabad.org)

Fill in the bagel with your "anything." Start with nothing and build your gratitude. Start with the empty hole of the bagel and work outward. Write a list of the little things in life that you are grateful for.

Proud Jew

Why do we thank Hashem, "Who did not make me a Gentile"? Should we not say it in a positive way, thanking G-d Who made us a Jew?

Hashem gives us free choice and it is up to us to live as a proud Jew. This is not something that just happens to us.

Why are you proud to be a Jew?

V'YEHI RATZON

וִיהִי רָצוֹן...שֶׁתַּרְגִּילֵנוּ בְּתוֹרָתֶךָ, וְתַדְבִּיקֵנוּ בְּמִצְוֹתֶיךָ, וְאַל תְּבִיאֵנוּ לֹא לִידֵי
חֵטְא וְלֹא לִידֵי עֲבֵרָה וְעָוֹן וְלֹא לִידֵי נִסָּיוֹן וְלֹא לִידֵי בִזָּיוֹן, וְאַל יִשְׁלֹט בָּנוּ יֵצֶר
הָרָע, וְהַרְחִיקֵנוּ מֵאָדָם רָע, וּמֵחָבֵר רָע, וְדַבְּקֵנוּ בְּיֵצֶר טוֹב וּבְמַעֲשִׂים טוֹבִים...

And may it be Your will...to accustom us to [study] Your Torah, and to
make us cleave to Your commandments. Do not bring us into sin, nor into
transgression or iniquity, nor into temptation or scorn; and may the evil
inclination not have mastery over us. Keep us far from an evil person and an
evil companion. Make us cleave to the good inclination and to good deeds...

As we begin our day, we acknowledge that although we may face
challenges and temptations from the evil inclination, bad thoughts,
friends, and neighbors, we have the strength to overcome darkness.

Ready, Set, GROW! ∼

- I am grateful for the strength to overcome the darkness.

- I am grateful to Hashem for bestowing kindness upon our people.

- I am grateful for the ability to remove negative words such as:
  I can't... It won't work because.. It's too hard because... I am not
  good enough. I am unworthy. I am a loser.

Reflect & Connect ∼

What are the dark words that create obstacles on your path to success?

BIRCHAT HATORAH

When it is dark, we fear. It is time to turn on the light.

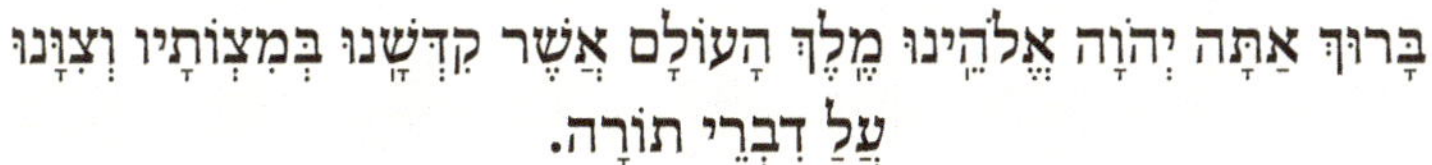

בָּרוּךְ אַתָּה יְהֹוָה אֱלֹהֵינוּ מֶלֶךְ הָעוֹלָם אֲשֶׁר קִדְּשָׁנוּ בְּמִצְוֹתָיו וְצִוָּנוּ
עַל דִּבְרֵי תוֹרָה.

Blessed are You, Hashem our G-d, King of the Universe, Who sanctified us with His words of Torah.

הַעֲרֶב נָא, ה' אֱלֹהֵינוּ, אֶת דִּבְרֵי תוֹרָתְךָ בְּפִינוּ וּבְפִי כָל עַמְּךָ בֵּית יִשְׂרָאֵל, וְנִהְיֶה אֲנַחְנוּ, וְצֶאֱצָאֵינוּ, וְצֶאֱצָאֵי עַמְּךָ כָּל בֵּית יִשְׂרָאֵ, כֻּלָּנוּ יוֹדְעֵי שְׁמֶךָ, וְלוֹמְדֵי תוֹרָתְךָ לִשְׁמָהּ. בָּרוּךְ אַתָּה ה' הַמְלַמֵּד תּוֹרָה לְעַמּוֹ יִשְׂרָאֵל.

And please, Lord, our G-d, make the words of Your Torah pleasant in our mouths and in the mouths of all of Your people, the House of Israel. And may we and our offspring and the offspring of Your people, the House of Israel - all of us - be knowing of Your Name and studying Your Torah for its sake. Blessed are You, Lord, Who teaches Torah to His people, Israel.

בָּרוּךְ אַתָּה ה' אֱלֹהֵינוּ מֶלֶךְ הָעוֹלָם, אֲשֶׁר בָּחַר-בָּנוּ מִכָּל הָעַמִּים
וְנָתַן לָנוּ אֶת תּוֹרָתוֹ. בָּרוּךְ אַתָּה ה' נוֹתֵן הַתּוֹרָה:

Blessed are You, Hashem our G-d, King of the Universe, Who gives the Torah.

Meditation

Your Divine Message

We are grateful we were chosen to teach that Hashem is the sole master of the world and to glorify His name.

Think of a great leader whose message changed the world. What if s/he did not share this message?

Close your eyes and visualize yourself on your mountain of Hashem, hearing His words and seeing the great Divine revelation.

What is your Divine message that you want the world to hear?

Visualize yourself sharing your Divine wisdom with your audience.

Who are they? What is their pain? What message do they need from you right now?

Ready, Set, GROW! ⟿

- I am grateful for the words of Torah, the light to dispel all darkness and overcome obstacles. Torah means "*hora'ah* - direction." I am grateful for the Torah, our guide and direction in life.

- I am grateful to Hashem for teaching us the Torah and for parents and teachers who make it pleasant.

- I am grateful to Hashem for His wisdom to transmit the joy of Torah to the next generation.

- I am grateful to Hashem for choosing us from amongst all the people of the earth to give us His most precious treasure anew every day.

Reflect & Connect ⟿

נוֹתֵן הַתּוֹרָה - Who Gives the Torah

Hashem is *"nosen haTorah,"* the one Who "gives" us the Torah in the present tense rather than in the past tense Who "gave," since the Torah is being given anew each day.

How do you experience Torah as a new gift each day?

Why are you grateful for the words of Torah?

"Meditate on Torah thoughts. A meditation rooted in a strong Jewish thought will push away negative thoughts."
—Rabbi Azriel Wasserman, o"bm

Choose a verse from the *Siddur*, *Tehillim* or *Tanya* that inspires and uplifts you. Contemplate and recite it in moments when your mind is free.

TORAH PASSAGES
IN PRAYER

The Torah blessings are recited for Torah study, so we are obligated to learn a bit immediately after reciting them. The selected Torah passages from *Chumash*, *Mishna* and *Talmud* have a common theme of kindness, good deeds, blessing and loving others, which the Sages have said is the basis of the whole Torah!

יְבָרֶכְךָ יְהוָֹה וְיִשְׁמְרֶךָ: יָאֵר יְהוָֹה פָּנָיו אֵלֶיךָ וִיחֻנֶּךָּ:
יִשָּׂא יְהוָֹה פָּנָיו אֵלֶיךָ וְיָשֵׂם לְךָ שָׁלוֹם:

And Hashem spoke to Moses, saying: Speak to Aharon and his sons, saying, 'Thus shall you bless the Children of Israel, saying to them: "May G-d bless you and guard you. May G-d shine His countenance upon you and be gracious unto you. May G-d turn His countenance toward you and grant you peace."

These three blessings are said in the merit of the three forefathers – Avraham, Yitzchok, and Yaakov.

Meditation

Hashem blesses you and protects you and your wealth or possessions. Visualize Him extending His protection over you and all that it is yours, including from the evil inclination.

Hashem makes His face shine upon you. Visualize Hashem opening your eyes to see your world with the light of the Torah shining upon you, illuminating your daily life.

Hashem lifts up His face and gives you peace. Think of something in your life that feels divisive, like two opposing forces. Visualize Hashem granting you peace and blessing for everlasting life in the World to Come.

Ready, Set, GROW!

- I am grateful that the *Kohanim* bless our nation during the *Musaf* prayers on the Holidays. In Israel, it is performed every morning.

- I am grateful for the blessings of wealth and protection.

- I am grateful for the light of Hashem that illuminates my life.

- I am grateful for the peace in my life.

Reflect & Connect

Before the *Kohanim* bless us, they recite: "Blessed is the One Who commanded us to bless the Jews with love." A *Kohen* is all about love. Every Jew is a *Kohen*[6] and has the ability to bless others with love.

---

6. *"You will be for Me a Kingdom of Priests and a holy people." Shemos 19:5-6*

When we bless each other, Hashem also blesses us and our cup overflows. Whom can you bless today? How will you bless them?

EILU DEVORIM

אֵלּוּ דְבָרִים שֶׁאָדָם אוֹכֵל פֵּרוֹתֵיהֶם בָּעוֹלָם הַזֶּה וְהַקֶּרֶן קַיֶּמֶת לָעוֹלָם הַבָּא,
וְאֵלּוּ הֵן כִּבּוּד אָב וָאֵם וּגְמִילוּת חֲסָדִים וְהַשְׁכָּמַת בֵּית הַמִּדְרָשׁ שַׁחֲרִית וְעַרְבִית
וְהַכְנָסַת אוֹרְחִים וּבִקּוּר חוֹלִים וְהַכְנָסַת כַּלָּה וּלְוָיַת הַמֵּת וְעִיּוּן תְּפִלָּה וַהֲבָאַת
שָׁלוֹם בֵּין אָדָם לַחֲבֵרוֹ וּבֵין אִישׁ לְאִשְׁתּוֹ וְתַלְמוּד תּוֹרָה כְּנֶגֶד כֻּלָּם:

These are precepts, the fruits of which man enjoys in this world, [while] the principal [reward] is preserved for him in the World-to-Come. They are: honoring father and mother, [performing] deeds of kindness, early attendance in the House of Study morning and evening, providing hospitality to guests, visiting the sick, participating in making a wedding, accompanying the dead [to the grave], concentrating on the meaning of prayers, making peace between fellow men and between husband and wife— and the study of Torah is equal to them all.

Ready, Set, GROW!

I am grateful for the *Mitzvos*, which give us pleasure in this world (as well as in the world to come):

- honoring father and mother

- [performing] deeds of kindness

- early attendance in the House of Study, morning and evening

- providing hospitality to guests

- visiting the sick

- participating in making a wedding

- accompanying the dead [to the grave]

- concentrating on the meaning of prayers

- making peace between fellow men and between husband and wife

- the study of Torah, which is equal to all these other precepts.

Reflect & Connect

How do you derive pleasure from these *Mitzvos*?

HAREINI

The Lubavitcher Rebbe started a campaign in 1983 for everyone to say "*Hareini Mekabel*" before *Tefillah* each day.

הֲרֵינִי מְקַבֵּל עָלַי מִצְוַת עֲשֵׂה שֶׁל וְאָהַבְתָּ לְרֵעֲךָ כָּמוֹךָ:

I hereby take upon myself the positive commandment of "You shall love your fellow like yourself."

Ready, Set, GROW!

- I am grateful for the ability to truly love myself and others — the basis of the entire Torah.

- I am grateful for my family and friends and for those who offer their love and friendship.

Reflect & Connect

We know we have faults, yet we still overlook them. Love others with their faults and take care not to expose them.[7] Instead of pointing out the flaws and correcting others, connect with them and pray for their success.

Hashem says: "My beloved children, do I lack anything that I have to ask you for? All I ask is that you love and honor each other."[8] With love and unity, we draw down the flow of blessings.

How can you take upon yourself to nurture your relationships with love and acceptance?

---

7. *Teaching of the Baal Shem Tov*

8. *Talmud, Bava Metzia*

ADON OLAM

Master of the Universe, Who reigned before any creature was created.

At the time when all was made by His will, then was His Name proclaimed King.

And after all things shall cease to be, the Awesome One will reign alone.

He was, He is, and He shall be in glory.

He is One, and there is no second to compare to Him, to associate [with Him].

Without beginning, without end, power and dominion are His.

He is my G-d and my ever-living Redeemer, the Rock of my destiny in times of distress.

He is my flag and my refuge;

He is the portion of my cup on the day I call.

Into His hand I entrust my spirit when I sleep and when I awaken.

And with my spirit my body, Hashem is with me, I shall not fear

אֲדוֹן עוֹלָם אֲשֶׁר מָלַךְ,
בְּטֶרֶם כָּל יְצִיר נִבְרָא.
לְעֵת נַעֲשָׂה בְחֶפְצוֹ כֹּל,
אֲזַי מֶלֶךְ שְׁמוֹ נִקְרָא.

וְאַחֲרֵי כִּכְלוֹת הַכֹּל,
לְבַדּוֹ יִמְלוֹךְ נוֹרָא.
וְהוּא הָיָה, וְהוּא הֹוֶה,
וְהוּא יִהְיֶה, בְּתִפְאָרָה.

וְהוּא אֶחָד וְאֵין שֵׁנִי,
לְהַמְשִׁיל לוֹ לְהַחְבִּירָה.
בְּלִי רֵאשִׁית בְּלִי תַכְלִית,
וְלוֹ הָעֹז וְהַמִּשְׂרָה.

וְהוּא אֵלִי וְחַי גֹּאֲלִי,
וְצוּר חֶבְלִי בְּעֵת צָרָה.
וְהוּא נִסִּי וּמָנוֹס לִי,
מְנָת כּוֹסִי בְּיוֹם אֶקְרָא.

בְּיָדוֹ אַפְקִיד רוּחִי,
בְּעֵת אִישַׁן וְאָעִירָה.
וְעִם רוּחִי גְּוִיָּתִי,
יְיָ לִי וְלֹא אִירָא.

This hymn has been attributed to Rabbi Shlomo ibn Gabirol, who lived in Spain during the eleventh century. While praising Hashem's omnipotence and providence, it clarifies the meaning of the name *Ad-o-noy* so that before proceeding to pray, each worshiper understands the significance of the Hashem he is addressing.

Meditation

"I Believe in Hashem"
Song by Rabbi Ephraim Wachsman

The first stanza of the song is as follows:

I believe in Hashem, I trust in Hashem
There never is a moment when
That I am alone, or on my own
I believe and I trust in Hashem

And I understand that He's holding my hand
And every step is perfectly planned
He's holding me tight, so I'll be alright
I believe and I trust in Hashem

Listen to the full version online:
https://www.youtube.com/watch?v=VhnLaJWN6cU

Ready, Set, GROW!

- I am grateful Hashem is always with me, and I shall NOT fear!

- I am grateful Hashem is my refuge. He was, is, and will be forever.

- I am grateful that I am never alone!

Reflect & Connect

"He is my flag:" It is to Him that I rally and through Him that I am identified.[9]

How are you a representative for Hashem on earth?

How does this prayer help you choose faith over fear?

––––––––––––––––––

9. *Etz Yosef*

STEP 2: RECOGNITION

Our Sages declared, "In the future, even though all things on earth will be in such an ideal state that there will be no more cause for prayers and offerings, prayers of gratitude and offerings of thanksgiving will nevertheless not cease.[10]"

The following sequence of prayers up to the concluding blessing "*Yishtabach*" is called *Pesukei Dezimrah*, or the Verses of Praise. This selection of Biblical passages was arranged by the *Gaonim* of the ninth century to fulfill the Talmudic dictum:

"A person should praise Hashem first and make his requests afterwards.[11]"

---

10 *Midrash Rabbah Tzav, 9*

11 *Talmud, Berachos 32a*

לעולם
ה דבר
נעלב
בשמים

BARUCH SHE'AMAR

בָּרוּךְ שֶׁאָמַר וְהָיָה הָעוֹלָם, בָּרוּךְ הוּא, בָּרוּךְ עֹשֶׂה בְרֵאשִׁית, בָּרוּךְ אוֹמֵר
וְעוֹשֶׂה, בָּרוּךְ גּוֹזֵר וּמְקַיֵּם, בָּרוּךְ מְרַחֵם עַל הָאָרֶץ, בָּרוּךְ מְרַחֵם עַל הַבְּרִיּוֹת,
בָּרוּךְ מְשַׁלֵּם שָׂכָר טוֹב לִירֵאָיו, בָּרוּךְ חַי לָעַד וְקַיָּם לָנֶצַח, בָּרוּךְ פּוֹדֶה וּמַצִּיל,
בָּרוּךְ שְׁמוֹ: בָּרוּךְ אַתָּה יְהֹוָה אֱלֹהֵינוּ מֶלֶךְ הָעוֹלָם הָאֵל הָאָב הָרַחֲמָן הַמְהֻלָּל
בְּפֶה עַמּוֹ מְשֻׁבָּח וּמְפֹאָר בִּלְשׁוֹן חֲסִידָיו וַעֲבָדָיו וּבְשִׁירֵי דָוִד עַבְדֶּךָ, נְהַלֶּלְךָ יְהֹוָה
אֱלֹהֵינוּ בִּשְׁבָחוֹת וּבִזְמִירוֹת נְגַדֶּלְךָ וּנְשַׁבֵּחֲךָ וּנְפָאֶרְךָ וְנַזְכִּיר שִׁמְךָ וְנַמְלִיכְךָ מַלְ־
כֵּנוּ אֱלֹהֵינוּ, יָחִיד, חֵי הָעוֹלָמִים מֶלֶךְ מְשֻׁבָּח וּמְפֹאָר עֲדֵי עַד שְׁמוֹ הַגָּדוֹל: בָּרוּךְ
אַתָּה יְהֹוָה מֶלֶךְ מְהֻלָּל בַּתִּשְׁבָּחוֹת:

Blessed is He Who spoke, and the world came into being, blessed is He;
blessed is He Who maintains the creation; blessed is He Who says and does.
Blessed is He Who decrees and fulfills. Blessed is He Who has compassion
on the earth; blessed is He Who has compassion on the creatures; blessed
is He Who rewards well those who fear Him, blessed is He Who lives
forever and exists eternally; blessed is He Who redeems and saves, blessed
is His Name. Blessed are You, Hashem, our G-d, King of the Universe, the
Almighty, the merciful Father, Who is verbally extolled by His people,
praised and glorified by the tongue of His pious ones, and His servants, and
through the songs of David, Your servant. We will extoll You, Hashem, our
G-d, with praises and psalms; we will exalt, praise, and glorify You; we will
mention Your Name, and proclaim You—our King, our G-d. Unique One, Life
of the worlds, King, praised and glorified forever is His great Name. Blessed
are You, Hashem, King, Who is extolled with praises.

Meditation

Enjoy the Little Things

When something is brand-new, it gives us pleasure. After we have it for a while, we start to take it for granted and even complain about it. A first step to enjoying each day of life is recognizing the little things around us.

Close your eyes for a few minutes, then open them and look around. Pretend you have never seen any of the things before you. Using your five senses, 'look' at everything as if you were born today and are now experiencing it all for the first time. You don't take anything for granted. Describe what you sense. It's a new day. You can enjoy the little things.

Look at a flower with fresh new eyes. Describe what you see.

Ready, Set, GROW! ～

I Recognize:

- …Hashem creates the world with His words

- …Hashem says [what He will do] and does it

- …Hashem decrees and fulfills

- …Hashem creates the world

- …Hashem has compassion on the earth

- …Hashem has compassion on the creations

- …Hashem rewards

- …Hashem lives forever, redeems and saves us

- …Hashem: You are the King; You are the only G-d and the life of all worlds

Reflect & Connect ～

"Who maintains the creation; blessed is He Who says and does"

Hashem's saying and doing are synonymous and simultaneous as *Tehillim* 33:6 says, "By the word of G-d, the heavens were made."[12]

Hashem is constantly creating the world with words. We, too, create our life with the words we use. What words can you choose to strengthen the positive in yourself and others?

---

12. *Etz Yosef*

ASHREI

Happy are they that dwell in Your house; they will be always praising You. Happy is the people whose fate is such, happy is the people whose G-d is Hashem. A Psalm of praise by David. I will extol You, my G-d, O King; and I will bless Your name forever and ever.
Every day I will bless You and I will praise Your name forever and ever.
Great is Hashem and to be highly praised; His greatness is unsearchable.
One generation to another shall laud Your works and shall declare Your mighty acts.
The glorious splendor of Your majesty and Your wondrous works will I discuss.
Men shall speak of the might of Your tremendous acts; and I will tell of Your greatness.
They shall commemorate the fame of Your great goodness and shall sing of Your righteousness.
Hashem is gracious and full of compassion, slow to anger and of great mercy.
Hashem is good to all and His compassion is over all His works.
All Your works shall praise You, Hashem, and your righteous ones shall bless You.

אַשְׁרֵי יוֹשְׁבֵי בֵיתֶךָ עוֹד יְהַלְלוּךָ סֶּלָה:

אַשְׁרֵי הָעָם שֶׁכָּכָה לּוֹ אַשְׁרֵי הָעָם שֶׁיְהוָה אֱלֹהָיו:

תְּהִלָּה לְדָוִד, אֲרוֹמִמְךָ אֱלוֹהַי הַמֶּלֶךְ וַאֲבָרְכָה שִׁמְךָ לְעוֹלָם וָעֶד:

בְּכָל־יוֹם אֲבָרְכֶךָּ וַאֲהַלְלָה שִׁמְךָ לְעוֹלָם וָעֶד:

גָּדוֹל יְהוָה וּמְהֻלָּל מְאֹד וְלִגְדֻלָּתוֹ אֵין חֵקֶר:

דּוֹר לְדוֹר יְשַׁבַּח מַעֲשֶׂיךָ וּגְבוּרֹתֶיךָ יַגִּידוּ:

הֲדַר כְּבוֹד הוֹדֶךָ וְדִבְרֵי נִפְלְאֹתֶיךָ אָשִׂיחָה:

וֶעֱזוּז נוֹרְאֹתֶיךָ יֹאמֵרוּ וּגְדוּלָתְךָ אֲסַפְּרֶנָּה:

זֵכֶר רַב־טוּבְךָ יַבִּיעוּ וְצִדְקָתְךָ יְרַנֵּנוּ:

חַנּוּן וְרַחוּם יְהוָה אֶרֶךְ אַפַּיִם וּגְדָל־חָסֶד:

טוֹב־יְהוָה לַכֹּל וְרַחֲמָיו עַל־כָּל־מַעֲשָׂיו:

יוֹדוּךָ יְהוָה כָּל־מַעֲשֶׂיךָ וַחֲסִידֶיךָ יְבָרְכוּכָה:

They shall speak of the glory of Your kingdom and talk of Your might;

to make known to the sons of men His mighty acts, and the glory of the majesty of His kingdom.

Your kingdom is a kingdom for all ages and Your dominion endures throughout all generations.

Hashem upholds all that fall and raises up all those that are bowed down.

The eyes of all wait for You and You give them their food in its proper time.

You open Your hand and satisfy the desire of every living being.

Hashem is righteous in all His ways and gracious in all His works.

Hashem is near to all who call upon Him, to all who call upon Him in truth.

He will fulfill the desire of those who fear Him; He will also hear their cry and save them.

Hashem preserves all who love Him; but all the wicked will He destroy.

My mouth shall speak the praise of Hashem, and let all flesh bless His holy name for ever and ever. But we will bless G-d from this time forth and forevermore; praise You, G-d.

כְּבוֹד מַלְכוּתְךָ יֹאמֵרוּ וּגְבוּרָתְךָ יְדַבֵּרוּ:

לְהוֹדִיעַ | לִבְנֵי הָאָדָם גְּבוּרֹתָיו וּכְבוֹד הֲדַר מַלְכוּתוֹ:

מַלְכוּתְךָ מַלְכוּת כָּל־עֹלָמִים וּמֶמְשַׁלְתְּךָ בְּכָל־דּוֹר וָדוֹר:

סוֹמֵךְ יְהֹוָה לְכָל־הַנֹּפְלִים וְזוֹקֵף לְכָל־הַכְּפוּפִים:

עֵינֵי־כֹל אֵלֶיךָ יְשַׂבֵּרוּ וְאַתָּה נוֹתֵן־לָהֶם אֶת־אָכְלָם בְּעִתּוֹ:

פּוֹתֵחַ אֶת־יָדֶךָ וּמַשְׂבִּיעַ לְכָל־חַי רָצוֹן:

צַדִּיק יְהֹוָה בְּכָל־דְּרָכָיו וְחָסִיד בְּכָל־מַעֲשָׂיו:

קָרוֹב יְהֹוָה לְכָל־קֹרְאָיו לְכֹל אֲשֶׁר יִקְרָאֻהוּ בֶאֱמֶת:

רְצוֹן־יְרֵאָיו יַעֲשֶׂה וְאֶת־שַׁוְעָתָם יִשְׁמַע וְיוֹשִׁיעֵם:

שׁוֹמֵר יְהֹוָה אֶת־כָּל־אֹהֲבָיו וְאֵת כָּל־הָרְשָׁעִים יַשְׁמִיד:

תְּהִלַּת יְהֹוָה יְדַבֶּר־פִּי וִיבָרֵךְ כָּל־בָּשָׂר שֵׁם קָדְשׁוֹ לְעוֹלָם וָעֶד: וַאֲנַחְנוּ נְבָרֵךְ יָהּ מֵעַתָּה וְעַד־עוֹלָם הַלְלוּ־יָהּ:

Meditation

Squeeze your toes tightly, until you feel the tension. After counting to three, relax your toes and release the tension there. Notice the difference between tension and relaxation.

Now, tense your forehead, cheeks, and lips. Count to three and release the tension. Reflect on the difference between your previous feelings of tension and your present feelings of relaxation.

Shut your eyes and tighten them. Keep them closed, relax them, then tighten them again and relax them.

Finally, tense your back and shoulder muscles. Lift your shoulders up. After counting to three, slowly let them drop as you release the tension.

You now feel completely relaxed. You are so relaxed that you no longer sense the weight of your body. You no longer feel weighed down by the burdens of life.

Feel lighter as a soothing wave of relaxation flows over and through you.

Form your hands into fists until you feel the tension. Count to three. Then, slowly open your hands and release the tension, financial worries, stress related to anything physical.

Open your hands as wide as you can as you say:

"Hashem, you open Your hand and satisfy the desire of every living being."

Contemplate how Hashem cares for you and your family.

Acknowledge your total dependence on Him. Food is essential.

Hashem is involved in every last detail of our lives.

He provides all of our sustenance at the right time.

Recite:

"There is enough! Praise Hashem! I will bless Hashem from now and forever."

You transcend all worries and frustrations.

You feel calm and at ease.

"Ashrei" - How fortunate are we that Hashem's ringer is never down.

"Hashem is near to those who call upon Him, to all who call upon Him in truth."

Ready, Set, GROW! 〜

I Recognize…

- "The eyes of all wait for You [Hashem] and You give them their food in its proper time."

- How Hashem opens His hand and satisfies the desire of every living being. I recognize that He is just in all His ways and benevolent in all His deeds.

- That He watches over all those who love Him and will destroy all the wicked.

- That Hashem is all-merciful and does only good. Everything aligns with His master plan for the universe. Thus, everything that happens is bound to be ultimately good, regardless of how it may appear to me and even when I do not understand His reasons.

Reflect & Connect 〜

Our Sages taught, "Whoever says Psalm 145 (*Ashrei*) three times daily will have a share in the World to Come." *Ashrei* demonstrates the unique nature of Jewish faith, in which our praise of Hashem is unconditional and everlasting.

Ashrei opens, "Happy are they that dwell in Your house; they will be always praising You. Happy is the people whose fate is such, happy is the people whose G-d is Hashem."

Ashrei concludes, "But we will bless G-d from this time forth and forevermore; praise You, G-d."

These verses teach us that the Jewish view of Hashem differs from that of other peoples in the conception of His Providence and mercy. "Don't be like others, who honor their deities when they fare well and curse them when they suffer bad luck," Rabbi Akiva called to the Jewish people. "You are Jews. When G-d brings you happiness, praise Him, and when you are suffering, praise Him, too."[13]

We conclude with the statement that Israel will never stop praising Hashem's glory, until "all flesh will bless His holy Name forever and ever."

How does the Jewish view of Hashem differ from other nations and how do you see it in your life?

13. Adapted from "My Prayer" by Rabbi Nissan Mindel

HALLELUKAH

הַלְלוּיָהּ, הַלְלוּ אֵל בְּקָדְשׁוֹ, הַלְלוּהוּ בִּרְקִיעַ עֻזּוֹ: הַלְלוּהוּ בִּגְבוּרֹתָיו, הַלְלוּהוּ כְּרֹב גֻּדְלוֹ: הַלְלוּהוּ בְּתֵקַע שׁוֹפָר, הַלְלוּהוּ בְּנֵבֶל וְכִנּוֹר: הַלְלוּהוּ בְּתֹף וּמָחוֹל, הַלְלוּהוּ בְּמִנִּים וְעֻגָב: הַלְלוּהוּ בְצִלְצְלֵי שָׁמַע: הַלְלוּהוּ בְּצִלְצְלֵי תְרוּעָה: כֹּל הַנְּשָׁמָה תְּהַלֵּל יָהּ הַלְלוּיָהּ: כֹּל הַנְּשָׁמָה תְּהַלֵּל יָהּ הַלְלוּיָהּ:

Hallelukah, Praise the Lord! Praise G-d in His Holiness. Praise Him in the firmament of His strength. Praise Him for His mighty acts. Praise Him according to His abundant greatness. Praise Him with the call of the shofar; Praise Him with a harp and lyre. Praise Him with timbrel and dance. Praise Him with stringed instruments and flute. Praise Him with resounding cymbals. Praise Him with clanging cymbals. Let every soul praise the Lord. Praise the Lord.

Meditation

This Psalm lists thirteen different instruments and musical tones with which we praise Hashem. Each instrument represents a different "tone," or time period in our life:

The powerful blast of the shofar resembles a time of crisis.

The delicate, soothing Kinor (harp) represents the quiet and serene periods of life.

The loud, exciting tof (drum) represents the pressured, hustle-bustle days.

The mournful chayil (flute) alludes to times filled with fear or sadness.

The happy-sounding cymbals represent the joyful celebrations.

At all these times, in all these moods, we search to find Hashem in our hearts and sing to Hashem.[14]

---

14 Rabbi Moshe Cordovero from Reaching New Heights by Miriam Yerushalmi

Ready, Set, GROW!

- I recognize that both the highs and lows in life are from Hashem and part of His plan.

- I recognize that I can choose to respond to any situation with song and praise.

Reflect & Connect

"There are chambers in heaven that can only be opened through song."[15]

Sing your prayers and feel your heart open.

What is your favorite song to sing while praying?

---

15 The Zohar

AZ YASHIR

אָז יָשִׁיר־מֹשֶׁה וּבְנֵי יִשְׂרָאֵל אֶת־הַשִּׁירָה הַזֹּאת לַיהֹוָה וַיֹּאמְרוּ לֵאמֹר אָשִׁירָה
לַיהֹוָה כִּי־גָאֹה גָּאָה סוּס וְרֹכְבוֹ רָמָה בַיָּם: עָזִּי וְזִמְרָת יָהּ וַיְהִי־לִי לִישׁוּעָה זֶה
אֵלִי וְאַנְוֵהוּ אֱלֹהֵי אָבִי וַאֲרֹמְמֶנְהוּ:

Then Moshe and the Children of Israel sang this song to Hashem, and they spoke, saying: "I will sing to Hashem for He is most high; a horse with its rider, He cast into the sea. The Eternal's strength and His vengeance were my salvation; this is my G-d, and I will glorify Him [make Him a dwelling-place]; the G-d of my father, and I will exalt Him."

Meditation

Our Most Sacred and Holy Dance

By Terri Klein, from her book
Mind Unlocked

Music can be so spiritually uplifting,
and often soothes the soul.
Closing my eyes I allow it to
transport me
to a place where I feel whole.

Dance has its own kind of magic,
with its beauty and its grace.
Allowing movement to flow through
me,
I create my very own sacred space.

Dancing with G-d
is my new-found love.
All I do is follow;
my moves are guided from above.

Faith is a decision;
becoming partners with G-d is a
choice.
Prayer affirms that very faith,
allowing the expression of my inner
voice.

When I arise,
each and every day,
my very first impulse
is to use the Gift of My Words to pray.

Thy will be done, Dear G-d,
I am here to serve only You.
Please show me what it is
that you would have me do.

Dance with me, Divine Partner,
and I will gladly follow your lead.
Although I may not always receive
what I want,
I trust that I will be given exactly
what I need.

Guide my footsteps, my words,
my thoughts, and my way.
And thank You in advance for all of
the miracles
that will be scattered throughout my
day.
Although I love to co-create,
I trust in You to conduct the show.
Simply direct me, one step at a time,
towards where I need to go.

I promise to pay close attention
to all of the messages that You send.
I will be open-minded to Your will
and, if necessary, I will bend.

After all, we are dancing
to the rhythm and music of life.
And knowing that You are leading,
seems to comfort any strife.

*Dear G-d, I pray for knowledge of
Your will*
and the power to carry it through.
*Show me how to be Your loyal
messenger,*
*for I would love to collaborate with
You.*

Talk to me through people;
*reach me through the "synchronistic
flow."*
Show me how to dance with grace,
and I promise to surrender and let go.

*I will accept Your no's, as well as
Your yeses;*
*I will have faith in Your Grand
Design—*
always inherently trusting
there is a lesson that I shall find.

Dear G-d, I do believe
that our dreams can coincide,
but please do not lose faith in me,
should I ever doubt or hide.

In time I will return
to dance my dance with You,
for I am one of the many partners,
whom You are working through.

With You by my side,
I feel so safe and sound,
and trust in Your guidance,

towards my Higher Ground.

So choreograph my dance,
for I am ready to receive,
as in Your Higher Power,
with all my heart I do believe.

I surrender to Your perfection,
as with the timing of the seasons.
*So, too, will I trust in Your Divine
timing for me,*
without question, doubt, or reasons.

Why something has happened
may not be clear or understood;
*I will simply have faith in the
knowledge*
that everything happens as it should.

For I am Your faithful partner,
so let us whirl and spin together.
Through rain or shine we will dance,
as our song lasts forever.

*With You, Dear G-d, all things are
possible;*
*I feel empowered and unlimited by
Your side.*
*As we dance, please embrace me
with arms open wide.*

*I promise to be patient and pay
attention,*
and I promise never to make haste,

for I do not want to miss that "something better,"
which may be born from grace.

You are my inspiration,
and will forever be.
Please allow me to be one of Your instruments,
and shine some of Your light through me.

For our love affair is eternal,
and based on unconditional faith.
It is a spiritual connection
that nothing can replace.

One more note before I finish,
please accept the genuine quality of my words.
I trust that my sincerity
can be felt as well as heard.

I intend to follow Your "G-u-i-dance";
"G-d," "u," and "i" will "dance."
I promise not to let You down,
so please, give me the chance.

And when I go to bed,
before sleeping for the night,
I shall thank You for our dance today,
for it truly will have felt so right.

Your Faithful Partner and Constant Companion

Ready, Set, GROW!

I recognize and praise Hashem for the miracles that He performed for our forefathers when they departed from Egypt and for miracles today.

Reflect & Connect

זֶה אֵלִי וְאַנְוֵהוּ - **This is my G-d and I will glorify Him**

These words may also be interpreted to mean: When I recognize and describe Hashem as if I am pointing my finger at Him, I can proclaim, "*This* is my G-d; He and I are CONNECTED as one!"

How can you glorify Hashem through beautifying a Mitzvah or sharing a miracle story with others?

STEP 3: ONENESS

You expressed gratitude.

You recognized and praised Hashem.

Hashem loves and sustains you.

Your heart is open.

Your soul is yearning for Oneness with its source.

SHEMA YISROEL

The *Shema* is a declaration of our faith in the One G-d, Hashem. He is our partner and His will is our will. The obligation to recite the *Shema* is separate from the obligation to pray and a Jew is obligated to say *Shema* in the morning and at night.[16]

שְׁמַע יִשְׂרָאֵל ה׳ אֱ-לֹהֵינוּ ה׳ אֶחָד

Hear, O Israel, the L-rd is our G-d, the L-rd is One

Meditation

שְׁמַע יִשְׂרָאֵל ה׳ אֱ-לֹהֵינוּ ה׳ אֶחָד

Hear, O Israel, the L-rd is our G-d, the L-rd is One

I take a moment to listen. To notice those moments that seem so separate from

16. Devarim 6:7

Hashem. Those feelings that seem so conflicting. Allow them to be, and feel them as they are. If they are truly from Hashem, it is all equal, there is no reason to fear. They are the gifts that are wrapped and concealed.

I look inward and find the essential truth behind the situation. Accept the oneness of Hashem in all areas of my life. The places beyond my understanding, the parts of me that seem so fragmented.

בָּרוּךְ שֵׁם כְּבוֹד מַלְכוּתוֹ לְעוֹלָם וָעֶד

Blessed be the name of the glory of His kingdom forever and ever.

Hashem is a partner in every step of this journey. He is in the sunrise and sunset, the missed opportunities and waiting places. The birds that chirp and in all my inner noise. I recognize Hashem in all the details of my life.

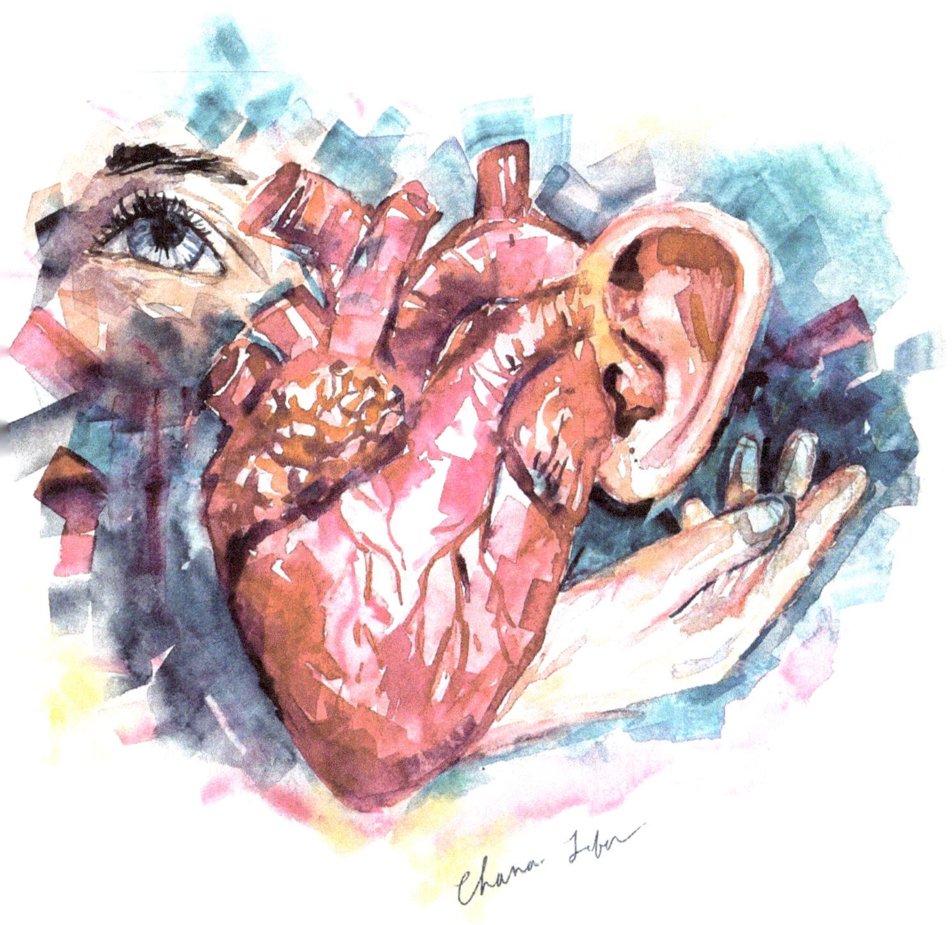

וְאָהַבְתָּ אֵת ה' אֱ-לֹהֶיךָ בְּכָל לְבָבְךָ וּבְכָל נַפְשְׁךָ וּבְכָל מְאֹדֶךָ

You shall love the L-rd your G-d with all your heart, with all your soul, and with all your might

I love Hashem with all my heart, all my soul and all my possessions, all that I am. There is no inner conflict, no fear. My mind and heart are one, open to receive Hashem's love. I am part of His oneness.

וְנָתַתִּי מְטַר אַרְצְכֶם בְּעִתּוֹ יוֹרֶה וּמַלְקוֹשׁ וְאָסַפְתָּ דְגָנֶךָ וְתִירֹשְׁךָ וְיִצְהָרֶךָ

I will give the rain of your land in its season, the first rains and the last rains, so that you can gather in your grain, your wine, and your oil.

Like the sprouting of a seed, my heart is sprouting love of Hashem. The seeds implanted in my mind and thoughts sprout healthy emotions.

אֲנִי ה' אֱ-לֹהֵיכֶם

I am Hashem, Who took you out of Egypt

I am FREE to break through all obstacles with Hashem's help and love today.

אֱמֶת *- True:*

I am free to be my TRUE self and spread TRUTH!

Repeat twice a day!

Ready, Set, GROW!

Visualize the Hebrew letter *Alef.* Its shape symbolizes how I reach up to Hashem and He reaches down to me. In reciting the *Shema,* I accept my mission to reveal Hashem's Oneness. This is Hashem's will. Hashem created a world of opposites in order for us to create oneness. Hashem's

will is my will.

- I am one with Hashem in learning Torah and doing *Mitzvos*.

- I declare and reveal Hashem's Oneness in everything I do.

- I create Oneness and love with others.

- I am one with Hashem in my joy and sorrow.

Reflect & Connect

ה' אֶחָד - **Hashem is One**

Alef (א) = One: Hashem is one.
Ches 8 (ח) = Hashem fills the 7 heavens and 1 earth
Daled 4 (ד) = Hashem fills the 4 corners of the earth

You feel love and connection.

With all your heart, soul and might.

Your world is filled with light.

How do you reveal Hashem's Oneness and bring heaven down to earth?

How do you grow your feelings of love for Hashem?

How do you connect in true Oneness with Hashem and others?

How do you show up when you OWN your faith and emotions?

STEP 4: WISHES

In the *Shema*, we expressed the desire of our soul to bond with Hashem:

"Your will is my will. Hashem is One."

Now, we turn our attention to our material needs.

In the *Shemoneh Esrei - Amidah*, we express to Hashem:

"Let my will become Your will, for we are truly ONE!"

We seek to draw down the Divine Blessings in order to create a dwelling place for Hashem in our world.

SHEMONEH ESREI - AMIDAH

Before the *Amidah*, we recall how our newly-freed ancestors praised Hashem's great name with a song at the seashore, after which we declare:

בָּרוּךְ אַתָּה יְהֹוָה גָּאַל יִשְׂרָאֵל

Blessed are You, Hashem, Who redeemed the Children of Israel!

We are confident that just as Hashem helped us in the past, He will continue to help us in every generation and bring *Geulah* — the Redemption!

Our faith in the Redeemer of Israel, Who redeemed us from Egypt, gives us the spiritual energy, courage and confidence to stand before Hashem, to pray and beseech Him for our needs as we proceed to the *Amidah*.[17]

אֲדֹנָי שְׂפָתַי תִּפְתָּח וּפִי יַגִּיד תְּהִלָּתֶךָ

My Master, open my lips, and my mouth will declare Your praise.

Meditation

Pre-Amidah Meditation

Take deep breaths and close your eyes.
Visualize Hashem speaking through you when you express your wishes.
"Hashem, open my lips so my mouth may declare Your praise."
Take another deep breath.
Exhale and count, 1…2…3…4…

---

17. *Yesodos HaTefillah*

Think of your soul that yearns to be one with Hashem.
Feel your breath.
Feel your heart.
Think of your wishes.
Think of your dreams.
Think of a miracle you are waiting to see.
Don't limit your opportunities.
You are a Lamplighter adding light around you.
Smile widely to yourself with your eyes closed.
In your heart, feel confident in Hashem's kindness and blessings.
"May the words of my mouth and the thoughts of my heart find favor before
You, Hashem, My Rock and my Redeemer."

Ready, Set, GROW!

The nineteen blessings of the *Shemoneh Esrei* prayer are divided into three primary sections. It is also known as the *Amidah,* since we "stand" in Oneness with Hashem to express our wishes and needs in order to serve Him fully. We recommend referring to a *Siddur* for the complete text of the prayer.

The first three blessings state the fundamental beliefs of Judaism in the one true G-d.

Recognition for:

- The great G-d of our forefathers, Who shields Avraham.

- The Almighty and powerful One, Who causes all events to happen, including the resurrection of the dead.

- G-d is holy

Wishes:

Personal wishes:

- For understanding

- For a state of closeness with G-d

- Forgiveness

- Deliverance from pain and strife

- Healing

- Good and plentiful produce

Communal wishes:

- For the reunion of Israel

- The Jewish judges shall return to rule

- The defeat of our enemies, informers and traitors (this blessing is actually the 19th, added by the Sages during the Roman occupation)

- The pious should be rewarded

- The rebuilding of Jerusalem

- *Moshiach* should arrive

Wishes regarding service to Hashem:

- Our prayers should be heard and accepted (many insert personal wishes here)

- For the Holy Temple and its service to be restored

- Thanksgiving for Hashem's mercies, for keeping us alive and providing for us constantly

- Grant peace and goodness in our lives

SHEMA KOLEINU

שְׁמַע קוֹלֵנוּ יְיָ אֱלֹהֵינוּ, אָב הָרַחֲמָן, רַחֵם עָלֵינוּ, וְקַבֵּל בְּרַחֲמִים וּבְרָצוֹן אֶת תְּפִ־
לָתֵנוּ, כִּי אֵל שׁוֹמֵעַ תְּפִלּוֹת וְתַחֲנוּנִים אָתָּה, וּמִלְּפָנֶיךָ מַלְכֵּנוּ רֵיקָם אַל תְּשִׁיבֵנוּ.
כִּי אַתָּה שׁוֹמֵעַ תְּפִלַּת כָּל פֶּה. בָּרוּךְ אַתָּה יְיָ, שׁוֹמֵעַ תְּפִלָּה.

Hear our voice, Hashem our G-d; merciful Father, have compassion upon

us and accept our prayers in mercy and favor, for You are G-d who hears

prayers and supplications; do not turn us away empty-handed from You,

our King, for You hear the prayer of everyone.

Blessed are You, L-rd, who hears prayer.

Meditation

Shema Koleinu Song

Composed by Ezra Eliyahu and Avrumi Fogel
Lyrics by Malky Giniger and Pinchas Eliyahu

Help me grow, to see, trust and know

Shema Koleinu, Hashem Elokeinu Chus Vrachem, Vrachem Oleinu

Father, can You hear me?

I know You're always there

Yet I'm lost throughout this journey

And life seems so unclear

Help me grow, to see, trust and know

Hashem, don't hide Your face from me no more

Father, hold me closer and show me the way

Through the times when it feels hopeless

I cry out and I pray
Hashem, help and guide me to climb and to strive
Help my heart and soul remain alive

Ready, Set, GROW!

I wish for Hashem to hear our voice and accept our prayers with mercy and favor.

Reflect & Connect

One Voice

In *Shema Koleinu,* we recite, "Hear our voice," and not "Hear our voices" in the plural form. Why?

Our private and unique voices merge together into one voice, weaving a magnificent tapestry of gratitude, heartbreak, recognition, song, tears, grief, frustration, praise, oneness, wishes, dance and growth.

We trust that Hashem will hear each one of our wishes because we are one voice. We pray for each other. We care for each other. We hold space for each other.

What is your wish for yourself or someone else? Use your Hebrew name and your mother's name. Talk to Hashem in your own words. Ask Him to bring your wishes into the physical realm.

Visualize your answered prayers and the joy and blessings you will experience. Praise and thank Hashem in advance for providing you with your needs in the right time.

TEHILLIM

שִׁיר לַמַּעֲלוֹת אֶשָּׂא עֵינַי אֶל־הֶהָרִים מֵאַיִן יָבֹא עֶזְרִי: עֶזְרִי מֵעִם יְהֹוָה עֹשֵׂה שָׁמַיִם
וָאָרֶץ: אַל־יִתֵּן לַמּוֹט רַגְלֶךָ אַל־יָנוּם שֹׁמְרֶךָ: הִנֵּה לֹא־יָנוּם וְלֹא יִישָׁן שׁוֹמֵר יִשְׂרָאֵל:
יְהֹוָה שֹׁמְרֶךָ יְהֹוָה צִלְּךָ עַל־יַד יְמִינֶךָ: יוֹמָם הַשֶּׁמֶשׁ לֹא־יַכֶּכָּה וְיָרֵחַ בַּלָּיְלָה: יְהֹוָה
יִשְׁמָרְךָ מִכָּל־רָע יִשְׁמֹר אֶת־נַפְשֶׁךָ: יְהֹוָה יִשְׁמָר־צֵאתְךָ וּבוֹאֶךָ מֵעַתָּה וְעַד־עוֹלָם:

A song of ascents: I shall raise my eyes to the mountains, from where
will my help come? My help is from Hashem, the Maker of heaven and
earth. He will not allow your foot to falter; Your Guardian will not slumber.
Behold, the Guardian of Israel neither slumbers nor sleeps. Hashem is your
Guardian; Hashem is your shadow, by your right hand. By day, the sun will
not smite you, nor will the moon at night. Hashem will guard you from all
evil; He will guard your soul. Hashem will guard your going out and your
coming in from now and to eternity.

Let's GROW!

Poem based on Chapter 121 of Tehillim
By Elisheva Resnick and Maital Ledder

Hashem is accompanying us
In Him we fully trust

We are **grateful**, never alone
He know that Hashem will lead us home

Wherever that may be
Hashem will set us free

"To the mountains I shall raise my eyes" (121:1)
And Hashem's help I **recognize**

In the dark of night or the light of day
We are **one**, Hashem is leading the way

"Hashem is your shadow," (121:5)
Even if we may be feeling low

"He will guard your soul" (121:7)
Helping us to reach our goal

We **wish** with Hashem to connect
As we *Daven* and reflect

"[He is] by your right hand" (121:5)
Even when we don't quite understand

Which way to turn or where to go
Every situation is for us to **GROW**!

HAYOM YOM REFLECTIONS ON TEFILLAH

Climb the Ladder to Connection!

Hayom Yom, Kislev 5:

"Behold, a ladder was standing on the ground."[18] *Prayer is the ladder by which the soul is bound to G-dliness. Though it "stands on the ground," for prayer begins with a simple acknowledgment of G-d, "its top reaches up to Heaven" [bringing a person to Onesses, which is called] a state of bittul atzmi. One arrives at this by first attaining an understanding of Pesukei Dezimra, the blessings that frame the Shema, and the recital of Shema.*

Hayom Yom, Tammuz 5:

One of the Alter Rebbe's prominent chassidim received a private audience, in the course of which the Rebbe inquired after his situation. The chassid complained bitterly that his financial situation had utterly deteriorated. The Rebbe responded: "You are needed to illuminate your environment with Torah and avoda of the heart - davening.

"Livelihood and what you need - that, G-d must provide for you. You do what you must, and G-d will do what He must."

---

18. *Bereishis 28:12*

What do you want from Hashem so you can illuminate the world with Torah and *Tefillah*?

Prayer: Language of the Soul

"I'm not in the mood to pray."

How many times have we heard that from our kids, our students, and even (gasp!) ourselves?

Nechama Laber, founder and global director of Jewish Girls Unite, suggests that this does not mean that we do not want to pray, but rather that "we are done praying without meaning."

"Prayer is the language of the soul," she says, then relays the familiar parable of the prince sent from the palace and forgets the language of his hometown. When he returns, he cries out from the depths of his soul and the king immediately recognizes him. "Sometimes, we are like that prince," Laber explains. "We forget the language of prayer. We become so entrenched in the worry, anxiety, and scarcity mentality of our daily lives that we forget the language of emotional connection with our Creator."

She has always been passionate about connection and credits her mother, Daniella Katzenberg, who exemplifies constant *Tefillah* for her children, and her father, Rabbi Azriel Yitzchok Wasserman o"bm, a beloved teacher whose approach she describes as "loving, vibrant, connecting." In 1974, the Lubavitcher Rebbe advised Rabbi Wasserman with three tips for connecting with his students:
- Words from the heart will enter the heart.
- Teach with joy.
- Be a living example to your students.

Recognizing students' strengths and encouraging their expression until he passed away at age 37 was "the way he always spoke," Laber recalls. "As I teach *Tefillah*, I find myself trying to bring back his voice and his language of connection that he taught me." An educator herself for 28 years and a certified life and trauma coach, she ties ideas back to Jewish sources: "It didn't take me long to see how everything in my own training is based in Torah. Now, we're bringing it home."

The GROW Method™ and The Connection Project

While teaching *Tefillah* to girls in the JGU Virtual School in early 2021, Laber planted the seeds of the method that would become the GROW Method™. It gained traction and developed in her women's group, Roses to Pearls (since 2014), who often explore the deeper meaning of selected prayers. Laber shared the idea with JGU Partner Micki Massry and this lead to collaborating on a way to honor the legacy of her mother, Claire Kosden-Perskie o"bm — a Holocaust survivor who exemplified faith, prayer, and family connection.

As the daughter of a renowned *chazzan* at Prague's *Altneuschul* ("Old-New") Synagogue before World War Two, a love for faith and prayer was instilled in Claire from her youth. Each day, she would recite the *Shema*, proclaiming faith in the One G-d; and each week, she kindled her *Shabbos* lights with personal prayers.

In her later years, Claire gathered her daughters Sheryl, Micki, and Ava, and asked, "Who will say *Kaddish* for me? Who will pray for me?"

Remembering Claire at a GROW Workshop for Educators in Massachusetts

"I will," Micki answered. "I will make sure we pray and say *Kaddish*."

Micki shared with Nechama that despite all the difficulties her mother lived through, she was the most loving mother to her daughters and their children. She spoke the language of connection, praying for them and showering them with praise and unconditional love. She wasn't bitter or angry because of all she endured.

"My grandmother loved life and when her grandchildren would visit she made sure they had a wonderful and interactive time with her. She would take us ice skating and golfing and to the beach. She accepted everyone and recognized our strengths. Most important to her was that we continue to follow along her path of connection to our faith," recalls her granddaughter, Julie.

Today, Micki often prays, honoring her mother's wish. She shared with Nechama her deep yearning to connect with the words of the Hebrew prayers more meaningfully. This desire, combined with stories of Claire's unwavering connection to faith and family, suggested a fitting legacy in The Connection Project and inspired the creation of The GROW Method™ at its core.

Jewish Girls Unite launched The Connection Project in August 2021 during their annual campaign, and it has since evolved into the GROW Connection Network. Amid fears, lockdowns and isolation around the pandemic, inspiration and human connection proved only more vital. Initially, The Connection Project aimed to address the anxieties and disconnect lingering from the pandemic by facilitating social, emotional, and spiritual connection based on Tefillah. Today, the Network empowers women and girls worldwide through GROW Connection Circles, mentorship training, creative tools and materials. These resources equip each person to give and receive and know she is not alone when she connects with her core, Creator, and community.

"Here, everyone of all backgrounds belongs. It is a judgment-free and safe space for moving from a place of disconnect to connection," says

GROW Mentor Terri Klein.

GROW Mentor Shaindel Leanse says, "When I come [to this group], I feel connected to the whole, to the Oneness in me."

Four-year-old Azriel Shepherd writing in his GROW planner

Suri, a Canadian participant in the Project, reflects: "I connected with women who empower me emotionally and spiritually. They help me clarify my wishes and show up as my authentic self. It has had an impact on my children. I hope we can give this connection to many more women and girls. It would be tremendous!"

Like *Tefillah*, the GROW Method™ is universal - for anyone of any age, personality or background. Four-year-old Azriel Yitzchok Shepherd, named after Rabbi Wasserman o"bm, echoes his great-grandfather's "language of connection" in his own GROW:

> G: I'm grateful for food to eat, my whole family, my clothes, my eyes, my eyeballs, my whole body.
>
> R: I recognize G-d who created the Rebbe, the sky, my brothers, toys, paper, Torah.
>
> O: To do Mitzvos, bring Moshiach and I own it by listening to Mommy, make Brochos and daven
>
> W: We hope Moshiach will come today! I Wish for spring tomorrow, my uncles to listen to me, and more markers.

The GROW Method™ proves an effective way of reviving the prayer experience by personalizing it, such as in the case of a young woman Laber coached: She had anxiety around prayer and for years refused to open a *Siddur*, so Laber first introduced GROW to her without identifying its basis in *Tefillah*. Afterwards, the client reported that she felt inspired and could start reconnecting via GROW. Her mother wrote, "[My daughter] seemed very at-ease and used the word 'inspired,' which I haven't heard from her in years. Thank You, G-d!"

GROW is Enhancing Interpersonal Communication

Not only is the GROW Method™ a way to enhance Divine connection, but many practitioners find it a highly useful tool for interpersonal communication for all relationships. Take the example of a woman in her mid-fifties, who attests, "[GROW] literally saved my marriage!" It makes sense that *Tefillah*, meaning "connection," translates into a daily language of communication with our families, children, partners, co-workers, anyone in our lives, says Laber.

Chaya Hott shares how she implemented the GROW Method to make a tough phone call to her daughter's teacher:

"About a week after I joined the GROW Connection Circle, I needed to make a phone call to my daughter's teacher. She had made one too many complaints and I just had enough. I took the plunge to call her and decided to use the GROW Method™. It worked like magic. Instead of having a confrontational conversation we had a very productive call and she even thanked me for calling

Laber with staff at Montreal schools after giving a GROW Workshop for students

her. How is that possible? I came with complaints! I was elated. Never did I have a conversation with complaints in such a productive way.

I explained to my girls that I had used the GROW Method™ and I explained how it worked. I don't talk about the GROW process all the time or even on a daily basis at all, but apparently I had planted a seed.

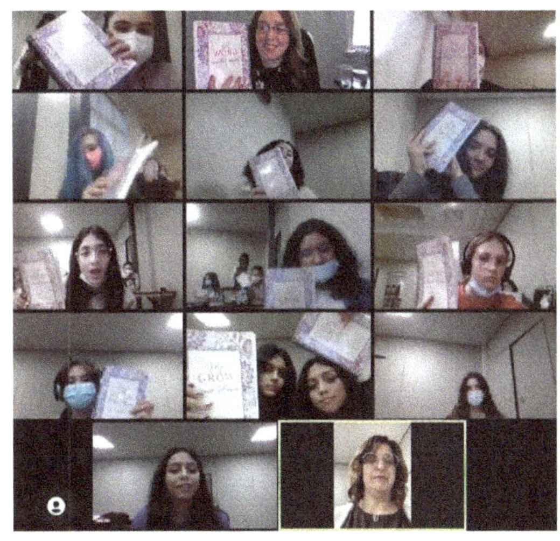

Online GROW Workshop with Planner for Bader Hillel High School students

Fast forward about three months later. My daughter notified me that her report card grades were incorrect, so she had approached her principal to have her change the grade. Some classmates were commenting how she must have a "special connection" with the principal—because she always gets what she wants from her. My daughter confessed, "I don't have a special connection; I just use GROW, and it works!"

As co-director of the Jewish Girls Retreat since 2000, Laber also implements the GROW Method™ in staff meetings: "I open up with Gratitude, thanking my counselors for all their hard work. Then I move on to Recognition, bringing up specific examples of ways they've been outstanding. I follow up with Oneness, how we're a team working toward the same goals. We take ownership to each do our part. Then we finish off with the Wishes for a successful camp experience." Communicating like this helps her counselors feel connected to their team and confident in their mission.

"GROW workshops at the Jewish Girls Retreat concretized spirituality and uplifted my eldest daughter, Adira," reflects Kate Friedman, a JGU mom in Florida. "I learned the ideas to help her maintain that high level and support my kids when they are overwhelmed. I can have a GROW conversation with them as they head out for school to help them center

JGU camper Adira Friedman prays by the lake

themselves and prepare to make prayer a meaningful, empowering part of their day. GROW is also useful for the transition from working hard in school to recharging at home, which isn't always restful for tweens or teens. I can remind my kids, 'G-d, You are the source of blessing. Please make me a vessel for Your light, and clear the path before me so I can magnify and share my gifts to develop myself, my family and community.'"

JGR Campers like Adira and JGU online students too are encouraged to start every program by practicing GROW, now facilitated by the JGU Press' *GROW Prayer Planner*, which is dedicated to Claire Kosden-Perskie. Between the attractive covers by the talented Carasmatic Design, the planner includes short reflections, writing prompts, and doodling space for users to apply GROW concepts to life.

Life's Better When We GROW Together

Women also enjoy the Planner, privately and online at GROW Connection Circles, which are small, moderated groups fostering inspiration and mutual support, using GROW-based multimedia content. One woman remarks, "Although I've prayed my whole life, I didn't know *how* to until I implemented the GROW Method™! I am amazed at the depth and creativity of your resources." Current Circles focus on *Tefillah*, growth challenges, parenting and intergenerational connection, with an eye toward expanding to newlyweds and to survivors of loss who want to memorialize a loved one's legacy.

At Shaindel Malka's GROW birthday farbrengen in California

One member of the *Tefillah* Circle, says, "My *Modeh Ani* will be very different from now on, not just lip-service." After reviewing GROW on gratitude via telephone with her Spanish-speaking community, a student remarked how the idea "reaffirms what she really believes." This initiative by women is the goal, explains Laber, who is training "GROW Mentors" to lead in their schools and communities.

Shaindel Malka Leanse, a GROW mentor from California, illustrated this beautifully by organizing a birthday *farbrengen* on the topic: "When you plow and sow, things will GROW" — a nod to the classic *Hayom Yom* for Cheshvan 25. While visiting California to conduct a GROW Workshop at Beis Chana High School, Laber joined the festivities to further address Leanse's guests on the topic.

GROW in the Classroom

GROW Workshops for Educators, envisioned by JGU Partner Shoshana Fox and sponsored by Refua Medicinals, offered coaching and collaboration in 2021. Laber hopes this will encourage schools everywhere to integrate GROW into their teaching philosophies in general and their *davening* practices in particular: "Just like we constantly upgrade our computer software, we can always advance our teaching methods."

Nechama and artist Chana Laber share GROW Prayer Planners and other JGU products at the Kinus Hashluchos resource fair

Through international tours and webinars, GROW has reached hundreds of educators, equipping many to facilitate deeper connection between teachers, students and their learning. From France to the United States, Brazil to the United Kingdom, and Israel to the Netherlands, classrooms are spiritually and emotionally more robust. GROW was also well-received at the distinguished Menachem Education Foundation Conference and the International Conference of *Shluchos* 5782/2022. Attendees loved the pilot version of *GROW Through Prayer* which led to the final publication by the JGU Press.

Following a GROW Workshop for educators at the Lubavitcher Yeshiva Academy in Longmeadow, Massachusetts, Director Rabbi Noach Kosofsky told Laber, "I look forward to implementing GROW in our school to further enhance the students' *davening* experience." LYA is currently in its second year of integrating the GROW Method™ in partnership with the GROW Connection Network.

Shterny Lew, an educator at the Yeshiva Schools of Pittsburgh and wrote to JGU: "GROW makes me so happy... This is brand-new for me to be teaching *davening*. I am so passionate about making it relevant and connected. [GROW] is a gift. I don't have time or resources to create, but I can execute!"

Lisse Gerofsky, who teaches at Chabad-Lubavitch of Markham, Ontario's Hebrew School, reported: "I introduced a very basic version of your amazing Planner to my [Torah Tots K-2] class. I have students with different types of backgrounds; they each respond at their own level. I

Laber gives a GROW Workshop for Educators at LYA

Giving a GROW Workshop to Bais Chana High School students in the synagogue in California

think this is one reason why personal journaling works so well. They shared some insightful entries and I'm so impressed with the way the older kids were able to link the four ideas [of GROW] together!"

Always an Opportunity for GROWth

Whatever one's age or background, communicating in the language of GROW requires a high level of consciousness: "It's hard to be in this zone when you're in flight-or-fight mode," notes Laber. "We want to train our brain daily to speak this language, and when we do, the long-term effect is self-regulation." It is possible for GROW to become one's second-nature, even in the most challenging situations, as Marnie Atias, a member of GROW Connection Circles, demonstrated:

"My father passed away yesterday. I'm so grateful that I've had my father all these years and for all the support he's given me in my life (Gratitude). I don't understand G-d's ways (Recognition), but I am leaning on Him and he will carry me through this hard time (Oneness). I'm hoping for the day when G-d will take away all suffering (Wish)."

The message was telling: "Life is not always perfect, but we can always turn it into a prayer and GROW through it."

When our forefather Yaakov, disguised as his brother Eisav, sought the

A guest at the Women's Connection Retreat kindles Shabbos candles with a personal prayer

firstborn's blessing, his father Yitzchak declared: "The voice is Yaakov's voice but the hands are Eisav's hands." According to the *Midrash*, Yitzchak insinuated that as long as the voice of Yaakov, the Jewish people, is raised in prayer, the hands of Eisav, our enemies, are powerless against us. We have historically witnessed the power of united and intentional *Tefillah* to shape hearts and events and lead into salvation. Today, as we are on the threshold of the final Redemption, we are called to take up our greatest defense: *Tefillah*, the language of connection with our core, Creator, and community.

Glossary

Heb. = Hebrew | Yid. = Yiddish

A"h - *Heb.* An abbreviation for "Alav/aleha hashalom - Peace be upon him/her," in reference to a deceased person

Avoda - *Heb.* Labor, work

B'ezrat Hashem - *Heb.* With G-d's help

Baruch Hashem (or B"H) - *Heb.* Literally, "blessed is G-d," similar to "Thank G-d!"

Bat Mitzvah - *Heb.* Literally, "Daughter of the Commandment"; a Jewish girl who has reached the age of twelve, becoming a Jewish adult Divinely responsible for keeping the commandments; the celebration marking this occasion

Berachos - *Heb.* Blessings

Bereishis - *Heb.* Literally, "in the beginning"; Genesis, the first of the Five Books of Moses

Bittul atzmi - *Heb.* Nullification of oneself

Chabad (or Chabad-Lubavitch) - *Heb.* Acronym for "chochmah [wisdom]," "binah [comprehension]" and "daas [knowledge]"; the Chassidic movement founded by Rabbi Shneur Zalman of Liadi in the later 1800s, centered in the Russian village of Lubavitch for over a century; of or relating to the Chabad-Lubavitch movement, a network of emissaries with centers stationed around the globe to disseminate Judaism

Chassid (pl. chassidim) - *Heb.* Practitioners of Chassidus, Hasidism, the 18th-century movement based on Jewish mysticism and founded by the Baal Shem Tov in Eastern Europe

Chazzan - *Heb.* A cantor, who leads a congregation in prayer

Chesed - *Heb.* Kindness

Cheshvan - *Heb.* The Hebrew month corresponding to October-November

Chizuk - *Heb.* Strength

Daven(ing) - *Yid.* Pray(ing)

Devarim - *Heb.* Literally, "words" or "things"; the fifth of the Five Books of Moses

Eishet Chayil - *Heb.* A woman of valor

Erev Shabbos - *Heb.* Sabbath eve; Friday afternoon

Farbrengen - *Yid.* A gathering addressed by a Rebbe or Chassidic leader; a casual gathering of Chassidim with singing and inspirational words.

Gaonim - *Heb.* Literally, "the magnificent ones"; the great Talmudic scholars of the Babylonian academies from 500 to 1038 C.E., who passed decrees, sent responsa and teachings throughout the Jewish world, and compiled many important Torah books

Gevurah - *Heb.* Strength, discipline

Hashem - *Heb.* Literally, "the Name"; G-d

Hashgacha Pratis - *Heb.* Literally, "detailed supervision"; Divine Providence, the concept in which G-d is directly involved in guiding the entire world.

Hayom Yom - *Heb.* An anthology of customs and insights for each day on the calendar, taught by Rabbi Yosef Yitzchak of

Lubavitch and compiled by his son-in-law, Rabbi Menachem Mendel Schneerson

Im yirtzeh Hashem (or IY"H) - *Heb.* G-d willing

Ka"h - *Heb.* An abbreviation for "K'aina hora - No evil eye," typically used in reference to one's blessings to dismiss envy, negativity or spiritual harm

Kaddish - *Heb.* Literally, "holy"; a brief prayer recited by a mourner or by the chazzan in a prayer quorum of ten or more men

Kavanah - *Heb.* Intention, focus

Kislev - *Heb.* The Hebrew month corresponding to November-December

L'Chaim - *Heb.* To life!

Midrash - *Heb.* The classical, homiletic teachings (individually or collectively) of our Sages on the Torah

Mitzvah (pl. Mitzvos) - *Heb.* Literally, "commandment"; one of the six hundred and thirteen Divine commandments in the Torah; also means "connection" from the Aramaic root of "*tzavsa,*" since *Mitzvos* connect us to G-d

Modeh Ani - *Heb.* Literally, "I give thanks"; the short prayer we say immediately upon awakening in the morning to thank G-d for restoring our soul and granting us a new day of life

Moshiach - *Heb.* Literally, "the anointed"; the Messiah, our long-awaited Jewish leader descended from King David, who will usher in the everlasting era of Redemption, universal peace and awareness of G-d

O"bm - An abbreviation for "of blessed memory"

Parshah - *Heb.* Literally, "section," a reference to the weekly Torah reading

Shabbos - *Heb.* The Sabbath

Shalom Bayis - *Heb.* Peace in the home, domestic harmony

Shema - *Heb.* Literally, to "hear"; the Biblically-mandated declaration of devotion to G-d and faith in His Oneness, recited daily in the morning and evening

Shevat - *Heb.* The Hebrew month corresponding to January-February

Siddur - *Heb.* Literally, "order"; a prayer book

Simchos - *Heb.* Joyful occasions, celebrations

Tallit - *Heb.* A ritual prayer shawl

Tammuz - *Heb.* The Hebrew month corresponding to June-July

Tefillah - *Heb.* Literally, "connection"; prayer

Tehillim - *Heb.* (King David's) Psalms

Tiferes - *Heb.* Splendor, beauty; mystically, it also stands for harmony and balance

Torah - *Heb.* Literally, "teaching"; the Five Books of Moses; the collective body of Jewish law, practice, tradition and teachings

Yerushalayim - *Heb.* Jerusalem

Yiddishkeit - *Yid.* Judaism

Acknowledgments

With much gratitude to:

Micki & Norman Massry,
Founding Benefactors, who believed in the vision.

JGU Press Team, who brought the vision into reality:

- Leah Caras, Graphic Designer

- Chana Laber, Artist

- Susan Axelrod, Global Strategy Advisor

The Connection Team, our first graduates of the GROW Leadership Masterclass, who were involved in envisioning, writing, editing and reviewing this book:

Lisse Gerofsky, Devorie Flohr, Terri Klein, Laurie Kaufman, Julie Knox, Shaindel Leanse, Chana Laber, Tzipporah Prottas, Karen Sarto (Dance leader at GROW Circles).

GROW Circle Gala Hostesses 2022, who show up weekly at GROW Circle and invite others to join our GROW Connection Network:

Chairwomen: Micki Massry & Julie Knox

Hostesses: Marnie Atias, Ahuvah Coates, Shternie Chanowitz, Aviva Bamberger, Devorie Flohr, Shoshana Fox, Kate Friedman, Terri Klein,

Laurie Kaufman, Shaindel Malka Leanse, Gittel Laber, Kimberly Ritz, Karen Sarto, Miriam Wolf, Chaya Hott, Malka Bracha Finkler, Sarah Freedman, Lisse Gerofsky.

With utmost gratitude to our Founding Donors 2021 and over 250 donors for your dedication to saving lives through meaningful connection!

You are listed with gratitude on our website.

Founding Donors: Micky & Norman Massry, Mishkan Yecheskel, Dr. Raphael Moshe & Shoshana Fox of Refuah Medicinals, Shloime & Mira Greenwald, Chananya & Sarah Rosenblum of TrafficTickets.com, Eli & Fraida Nash, Ory & Linda Schwartz, Arthur & Nanette Brenner, Mendy & Feige Gorodetsky, Azriel & Chana Wasserman, Asaf & Zelda Advocat, Yitzchok & Julie Gniwisch of Delmar Manufacturing, Shaindel and Shimon Leanse, Neil & Lisa Gildener, Jack & Ellen Kaplowitz, Mendy & Chaya Shepherd, Rochie Shemtov, Noach & Golda Wasserman, Motti & Masha Donat, Ben & Rachel Federman, Richard Polak, Loren Lichtenstein, Shaina Rahmani, Susan Lowenthal Axelrod, Dr. Steven Parnes, Marc & Judy Ehrlich, Chavi Goldberg of Cybersem.com, and Tali Salver.

SHOLOM & CHANA ZELDY
MINKOWITZ
in memory of everyone's favorite Zaidy,
R' AVRAHAM AARON
RUBASHKIN O"BM

DR. EDWARD & LAURA JACOBS
in memory of mom
PRISCILLA JACOBS, O"BM
*who lived with immeasurable faith
and endless love for Yiddishkeit.*

If we have mistakenly omitted your name, please let us know.

About the Author

Nechama Laber is the founder and global director of Jewish Girls Unite, an experienced educator, Judaic consultant, Bat Mitzvah mentor, curriculum designer, certified life and trauma coach, public speaker, and the author of *Finding Song in Sorrow*. Since 1996, she has co-directed Chabad of Southern Rensselaer County with her husband, Rabbi Avraham Laber, where they reside with their 11 children (ka"h) and run the beloved Jewish Girls Retreat.

About the Artist

Chana Laber grew up on *shlichus* in Upstate New York, where she discovered the power of art to inspire. Her work focuses on powerful messages of Torah and *Chassidus*, exploring all mediums of art. She teaches art, *Chassidus* and *Tefillah* online and in-person at girls' classes, paint-a-prayer workshops, and special events. You can follow her on Instagram @laberoflove.